the

PASSION
BELIEF
M · E · T · H · O · D

personal strengths and desires that can eliminate self-sabotage and help you to create an expansive life!"

—**SANDRA DEE ROBINSON**, Actress, TV host, author, speaker and CEO of Charisma on Camera Confidence Training andHorsepowered Consulting LLC
www.CharismaOnCamera.com

"Megan's book, Passion to Profits, is a brilliant, down to earth, and powerful guide on how anyone with real commitment can create the business they desire and achieve financial independence."

—**RUTH KLEIN**, best-selling author of *Time Management Secrets for Working Women* and *The Destress Diva's Guide to Life*

"This is a wonderful book for anyone that is seeking guidance in creating a fulfilled, passionate life and/or business that they love. It teaches powerful tips and strategies on how to uncover your unique brilliance and how you can utilize your value and gifts to help change the world!"

—**JILL LUBLIN**, master publicity strategist, international speaker and 3x best-selling author including *Get Noticed Get Referrals*

"Megan Tull has given us a book that not only helps you replace your limiting beliefs with empowering ones, while helping you get clear on your purpose, but she also guides you straight through the path to success. This path will lead you to creating a passionate and prosperous life and business."

—**ALLISON MASLAN**, Author, *Blast Off! The Surefire Success Plan to Launch Your Dreams into Reality*

"The *Passion Belief Method* offers a proven simple success formula to create a lifestyle business that reflects your unique value and your brilliance. You can have it all; a life full of passion, love, health, and fulfillment all while making a difference in the world, Megan can show you how."

—**TOM ANTION**, Internet Multimillionaire
and Consumer Advocate

"Simple and effective, this book will move you forward towards a life full of everything you want - passion, love, joy and fulfillment!"

—**KENDALL SUMMERHAWK**, Leading Expert in Women
Entrepreneurs and Money, WomenInCoaching.com

"Megan Tull not only demonstrates exactly what it takes to have passion, drive and perseverance to get the job done but explains it in a very simple to follow and achievable format in this fabulous book. I recommend picking up a copy for yourself and someone who you know needs to change their life forever, too!"

—**TONYA HOFFMAN**, CEO and Founder of the Public
Speakers Association www.publicspeakersassociation.com

"Working with Megan has been fabulous! I definitely experienced a transformation that has given my business a new and exciting direction. After being stuck for a while, it was just what I needed to move forward in a positive direction. Within a couple of days of the session, my new mindset brought in a very successful job and I was able to see immediate results from Megan's coaching. I'm now very optimistic about the future of my business and I'm looking forward to continuing with

Megan and having more breakthroughs with the Silverlining Success Mentorship 12 month Program."

—**ANNETTE MCCAUGHTRY**,
CEO of Papers to Pearls Organizing Solutions

"Owning a business can be overwhelming. At times it's easy to find yourself lost in the weeds, unable to step back and see the big picture. I understand this, which is why I hired Megan Tull as my business coach. Through her Mentorship Program, she has helped me sort through my professional obstacles and establish a "what" and why" for my business once again. Specifically, Megan has been instrumental in helping me establish my fees and value of services that I offer. Within a 60 day period I was able to double my revenue. Her motivation and positive spirit are her natural born gifts. Her Mentorship Program is well thought out with topics ranging from having a healthy relationship with money to structuring a business for success. If you are ready to commit to yourself and work hard both mentally and physically, let Megan guide you in that transformation."

—**NATALIE HOWE**, CEO of Natalie Howe Designs

Foreword by
Ruth Klein, Six Time Best Selling Author

the
PASSION
BELIEF
M · E · T · H · O · D

Own Your Value &
Earn Your Worth
IN BUSINESS

MEGAN TULL

New York

the PASSION BELIEF M·E·T·H·O·D
Own Your Value & Earn Your Worth IN BUSINESS

Published in New York, New York, by Morgan James Publishing. Morgan James and The Entrepreneurial Publisher are trademarks of Morgan James, LLC. www.MorganJamesPublishing.com

The Morgan James Speakers Group can bring authors to your live event. For more information or to book an event visit The Morgan James Speakers Group at www.TheMorganJamesSpeakersGroup.com.

ISBN 978-1-63047-594-9 paperback
ISBN 978-1-63047-595-6 eBook
Library of Congress Control Number:
2015935794

Edited by:
Richard Willett

Cover photo, back photo and author photo by
Amy Weison Photography

Hair Styling for Cover photo, back photo and author photo by
Shandi Nichelle

Cover Design by:
Rachel Lopez
www.r2cdesign.com

Interior Design by:
Bonnie Bushman
The Whole Caboodle Graphic Design

A free eBook edition is available with the purchase of this print book.

CLEARLY PRINT YOUR NAME ABOVE IN UPPER CASE

Instructions to claim your free eBook edition:
1. Download the BitLit app for Android or iOS
2. Write your name in **UPPER CASE** on the line
3. Use the BitLit app to submit a photo
4. Download your eBook to any device

In an effort to support local communities and raise awareness and funds, Morgan James Publishing donates a percentage of all book sales for the life of each book to Habitat for Humanity Peninsula and Greater Williamsburg

Get involved today, visit
www.MorganJamesBuilds.com

Habitat
for Humanity®
Peninsula and
Greater Williamsburg
Building Partner

To Andrew, Cameron, Lauren,
Ashley and to all that are aspiring to
achieve something amazing in their
lives and are ready to tap into their unique
brilliance, so they can reach their
true potential.

*"Be courageous, take inspired action
and share your gift with the world."*

—Megan Tull

CONTENTS

FOREWORD

There are few books that truly share the exact steps revealing how to increase your money mindset while identifying your passion, as well as a method for living and owning a purpose-filled life and business. Megan's book, "The Passion Belief Method," is a volume of inspiration for those who know they have a great gift to offer the world, but may not know where to go next, or where to find the tools and strategies that will truly make a difference in their lives and businesses.

Megan shares her courageous journey in an elegant and graceful way. Her approach to life and to business is shared through the wise lens of someone who has experienced loss, confusion, self-sabotage... only to find a true path to a blessed life and successful business.

Up close and personal, Megan shares what it takes to pull yourself up from a directionless track to a passion path, from low self-worth to highly valuing yourself and your brilliance and evolving from earning little money to exceeding your bold money goals.

Megan's chapter on serving rather than selling is alone worth the investment of purchasing and studying this book because it shows where your old money mindset is not presently working for you and can be changed to a whole new sales paradigm… something new for most conscious entrepreneurs.

The consummate entrepreneur, Megan captures this entrepreneurial spirit that only a truly successful female entrepreneur can share and lives by example. She has taken this carefully crafted information and converted it into a successful passion belief method for the reader.

"The Passion Belief Method" is for any entrepreneur who knows deep down that they have much to give and feels aligned with Megan's entrepreneurial spirit!

This book will not only speak to your rational mind, but also to your heart.

Much success!

Ruth Klein

Creative Brand Strategist & Productivity Coach

www.ExpertCelebrity.com

Six-time bestselling author of

"*Time Management Secrets for Working Women.*"

Featured in *O: The Oprah Magazine*

PREFACE

I'm so thrilled and honored to be fulfilling one of my longtime dreams, which is writing this book. My life has been full of many incredible experiences, all of which offered great learning opportunities and life lessons. I wanted to have the chance to share the amazing insight and knowledge that I've been blessed to gain during this process. This information is drawn from what I've learned in my personal and professional life, as well as through the work I've done with my hundreds of clients over the years.

Many male and female business owners struggle with realizing the unique value of what expertise or services they offer and lack confidence in accumulating and managing money. This often happens because when individuals are not crystal clear on the value that they provide, they do not have the confidence needed to earn what they're worth in the workplace. This prevents them from supporting themselves financially or sustaining their business. In order to make up for the low fees, they often end up working too many hours and get burned out, or they struggle with selling themselves or their products or services due to the underlying fear or doubt that shows up. Thoughts of "Am I good enough?" or "Am I worth it?" are disempowering and will sabotage their business success.

Because of this common unhealthy relationship with money, many individuals, especially women, remain underpaid employees or do not charge enough for their services.

According to Catalyst, the leading nonprofit organization to expand opportunities for women in business, in 2012 the median weekly earnings for full-time working women in the United States were $691 compared to $854 for men. That's 25 percent less!

The good news is . . .

Now is such an exciting time for entrepreneurs (especially women), as well as the *ideal time* to become an entrepreneur. We are starting to see tremendous growth in this area, as more and more individuals are transitioning into entrepreneurship. People are tired of the lack of flexibility in corporate America, their limited income potential, their unsatisfying work environment and the boredom of not being challenged enough. Statistics show that female business owners in particular will provide 5.5 million new jobs by 2018. For every ten men starting a business, eight women are starting one as well. The Kauffman Foundation, one of the largest foundations devoted to entrepreneurship, has decided that this is the decade for women to become entrepreneurs and seek advisors who will help with the transition in order to unleash their potential and help them to fundamentally change their lives.

With this tremendous opportunity for entrepreneurs, my book will provide the necessary tools to allow them to change their mindset around money, as well as provide strategies to reveal their value so they can move forward in confidence and create a highly lucrative career or business based on their passion and values.

I'm personally blessed to be living an amazing life. I have a wonderful and loving husband, Andrew, and three amazing children, Cameron, Lauren and Ashley, and two awesome pets, Flopsy, our dog, and Chloe, our cat. I'm so grateful that I get to do what I love each day and make a living helping people reach their true potential by discovering their brilliance. I'm not sharing this to impress you, I'm sharing this to inspire you. The truth is, my life was not always like this. In fact, I struggled for much of my life held captive by the many adversities that I experienced, such as overcoming the tragic loss of my first husband, who was my high school sweetheart. We met when I was fifteen years old and shared fifteen years together, before he so suddenly left this earth. I was a single mom for nine and a half years. I was in multiple unhealthy relationships and dealt with many financial hardships throughout those years. On the other hand, I've also experienced many successes in my life, such as starting and running seven successful businesses, raising three kids, living a healthy and fit life and helping thousands of individuals reach their personal and professional goals.

Through my faith, dedication and unwavering commitment to my goals and my mission, I was able to turn my life around. Over the years, I have developed systems and processes that I use today in my coaching practice, to help individuals create a money magnetizing mindset, so that they can turn their passion into huge profits. I created my Passion Belief Method—Five Steps to Your Empowered Self—which allows individuals to tap into an amazing inner power and strength that tremendously increases their self-worth and value, so they can move forward confidently with a new and empowering belief system. It also allows them to make their personal mark in the world, leave a legacy behind and make a difference.

Through this book, I would like to share what I've learned on my life's journey. My goal is to equip you with the tools and strategies to help you get through the challenging times in your life graciously. Additionally, you will have the ability to eliminate negative beliefs that are holding you back from reaching your true potential; to gain clarity on your unique gift, so that you can tap into your brilliance; and to identify your priorities and values, so that you can come into alignment with your true self, start living your purpose and create the life and business of your dreams.

This book is meant to be a complete guide to provide you with everything you require to develop a mindset for success, so that you can reach your personal and professional goals, your desired level of success, in all areas of your life. This book offers a success formula that focuses on living a life full of passion, love, integrity, health, joy and purpose, all while making a difference in the world.

You can read this book consecutively, chapter by chapter, which is what I strongly encourage you to do, as it will provide you with the most benefit. Or you can go to a specific chapter that focuses on a particular area that you may require some guidance in at that moment. You can also use this book as your go-to resource as you navigate through life and build your business, and possibly need to course correct from time to time.

As entrepreneurs, we can make a tremendous difference in this world. It is our responsibility to identify and develop our gifts, so that we can serve others and make this world a better place.

Are you ready to own your value and earn your worth and live the life of your dreams?

Let's get started!

Chapter 1

IGNITE YOUR PASSION AND CREATE A PROFITABLE BUSINESS THAT YOU LOVE

O ver the past twenty years as a student of personal growth and a business and life coach, I've been incredibly blessed to witness many individuals change their destiny by taking control of their futures and start to follow their dreams. This often means getting really uncomfortable. The problem is that most people go through their lives like zombies following the same routine day to day;

they almost get numb to it and go on autopilot. This is so sad to see; it's like they have no spark inside them; they're just a dull, lifeless being with no passion.

Take Control of Your Future

The great news is that you always have a choice to make: you can either stay stuck and continue on the same unfulfilling path to nowhere, or you can choose a different path, or—*even better*— you can create your own. However, it takes a very determined individual to step out and break free from his or her current life and create a different reality in life and in business. What often happens is that people are just trying to muster up enough energy to get through the day, and they get so caught up in their business or their life that they have a finite vision of what's real and what's possible. When you can't see beyond your daily calendar, it's hard to see what you've become and where you're headed.

People who create the life of their dreams and live their passion typically have these things in common: they're following a burning desire that no longer allows them to ignore their passion, and they're 100 percent committed to making significant changes and starting to take responsibility for their actions and their results.

Dolly Parton once said, "Find out who you are and do it on purpose." This book is a reflection of this. Throughout each chapter, you will get closer and closer to connecting with the inner passion that is unique to you and you will learn how to come into complete alignment with your true self, so that you can live your life with integrity, peace and joy. And the best part is that I will be here to help you every step of the way.

In order for you to ignite this passion, you must get clear on what you truly want. What are you passionate about? What really fires you up? This is what I like to call the "Ignite Your Passion Process."

The Ignite Your Passion Process

This is a process that I designed to assist you in starting to reveal and ignite your true passion.

Think about the following three questions:

1. What do I love to do?
2. What do I do that I can't help but do?
3. What do people tell me I'm good at or that I'm a natural at?

This will help to get your creative juices flowing. Next, start thinking about what you want your life and business to look like.

A Personal Experience Using the Ignite Your Passion Process

I once had a client whose name was Kathy. She was struggling to find direction in her life; she knew that she wanted something more, but she wasn't quite sure what that meant for her. She was in her mid-forties and told me that she felt that maybe it was too late for her to start over. I wanted to ignite Kathy's passion, so I went through my Ignite Your Passion Process with her. I asked her the three questions above. After I asked her the first question—"What do you love to do?"—she was able to come to the realization that she really loved nutrition and learning how what you eat or don't eat can affect the way you look and feel. She had struggled with her own weight for several years. She had been embarrassed at how she looked and had very little energy. Through educating herself on health and nutrition she was able to lose a significant amount of weight and felt ten years younger. She was very passionate about anything that had to do with health and nutrition. When I asked the second question—"What do you do that you can't help but do?"—she shared that she can't help but assist others with their health challenges and help them get healthy through proper nutrition and diet. Finally, when I asked her the final question—"What do people tell you you're good at?"—she mentioned that people were always telling her she should start a business counseling people on health and nutrition since she had so much knowledge about the topics and was so generous in helping others.

After I went through this exercise with Kathy, it became very clear that she was incredibly passionate about health and wellness and that she had a natural gift for helping others in this area. Following this exercise, Kathy made a decision that she would get a wellness coach certification so she could help other women who were struggling with their health and/or weight. She told me that she had never felt so sure about anything in her life.

It is never too late to find your passion and follow your dreams. We have all been blessed with incredible gifts. It is our responsibility to share those gifts. In some cases, due to life circumstances, schooling, kids, etc., our passion may temporarily be suppressed. However, when that spark inside ignites, don't ignore it; it's time to discover what it means for you.

When this became clear in my life, I had been working as a trainer and manager for an international skin care company for nine and a half years. At that time, I was the manager for the state of Florida. My responsibilities included working with new spas, from layout design to training the staff on product knowledge, treatment procedures, sales and marketing. I put on several seminars and trained attendees at many trade shows across the country. I also worked very closely with our local beauty distributor and trained their eighty sales consultants on our products. This position required a tremendous amount of traveling.

Then, suddenly, my whole world turned upside down. When I was thirty, I tragically lost my husband to an alcohol-related death. My son, Cameron, was two and a half at that time. Not quite ready to face the emotions that came with this significant loss, I threw myself into my work. The traveling continued, but I really started feeling guilty for not being there for my son when he needed me most. I realized that things needed to change. I couldn't bear to be away from him all of the time anymore. I had to get clear on my priorities and how I wanted my life to be. Once I made the very important decision to create a lifestyle-based business that allowed me to put my son first as my top priority, it was full speed ahead from there. Of course, I was scared, but my desire to be there for my son was so much greater than the fear. So that's what I focused on. Then, I had to think about what type of business I wanted to have. I had always loved helping people be successful, so I decided to go into the personal development field. I immersed myself in all the personal growth and business training I could get my hands on. I followed leaders who were already getting the results that I was committed to achieving—this gave me hope that I could do it as well. There was a substantial learning curve in marketing my new business. I knew nothing about Internet marketing, and now all of a sudden I had to become an expert in it, since the Internet was where I would be finding the majority of my potential clients. Despite all of the challenges, I was able to triple my previous income within the first year in business. This was the time of my life when I realized there was no going back. The opportunities of being an entrepreneur were unlimited and incredibly rewarding. I learned more about myself that first year in business than I ever had before. The cool thing was that with the financial success came a newfound confidence. With this confidence came some new and exciting financial and business goals.

The lesson here is . . . if you're scared—do it anyway. Let your "why," your passion, drive you and motivate you each day to move you closer to your goals. There were so many times that

I was completely frustrated, scared or even felt like giving up. During those times, I would just think of my son Cameron and our new life together, push through the frustration and fear and move forward.

In his book *Live Your Dream* Les Brown shares a simple yet very powerful message: "*We may not always be able to control what is put in our path, but we can always control what we are . . .and what we will become.*"

"Go For It" Formula—
Turn Your Dream Business into a Reality

Get unstuck. This starts with making a decision to change your situation. This takes a tremendous amount of courage. When you make this commitment / empowered decision, amazing things start to happen and opportunities present themselves.

Open your mind. There is a possibility that things can be different. Visualize a different life for yourself—a life that allows you to put your priorities first, to grow, to share your gift and lead a prosperous and abundant life.

Focus on what you're passionate about. (Go through the Ignite Your Passion Process on Page [3]).

Observe how your life is now. You must accept your life now before it's possible to move forward into a new reality. This means taking responsibility for the choices you made in your life up until now. This is incredibly powerful because once you accept that you're responsible for your past results, then you also realize that you're responsible for your future.

Realize your true potential. All human beings, regardless of background or past experiences, have the incredible capacity to accomplish far beyond what they think their limits are. Focus on your strengths. What skills or talent do you possess? Be sure to be grateful for opportunities.

Remember: Failures are only growth and learning opportunities.

Initiate a plan. A business or life plan is your road map to success. This will contain your Executive Summary (a snapshot of your business plan as a whole and how it touches on your mission and goals); a Company Description (which provides info on what you do and what differentiates your business from others in your target market); and finally, your Market Analysis (before launching your new business, it's essential for you to research your business industry, market and competitors).

Take massive action. I don't care if you have the best plan in the world, if you don't take massive action to go after what it is you want, you're never going to get where you want to be. By taking action, you will start to get results. When you get results, your confidence increases. It's common for many individuals to have old, limiting beliefs or fears show up. Even if you're afraid—do it anyway . . . it will get easier.

In the book *The Confident Woman Devotional* by Joyce Meyer, one of my favorite books, there is a great story about overcoming fear that I'll share with you. There was a woman, we will call her Annie, who literally lived in fear for most of her life.

It controlled her. She would not drive a car or go out at night. She was afraid of crowds, of meeting new people, new things, airplanes, failure and just about anything else you can imagine. Her fears entrapped and tormented her. She desperately wanted to be courageous and brave. She wanted to have an exciting life full of adventure, but her dreams were squelched by her fears. One day Annie shared her situation with a close friend, and her friend said simply, "Why don't you just do it *afraid*?" What an amazing and powerful truth! This was the beginning of a new life full of opportunity for Annie, all because she realized that she didn't need to wait for the fear to go away before she took action.

Don't let fear stop you. There are so many opportunities that are available to you that will enable you to live the life of your dreams, a life of passion and prosperity. My clients who have chosen to follow their passion, and the steps necessary to design the life of their dreams, have found a new sense of purpose in their life and business.

Forbes magazine states that a quiet revolution is taking place right now among women. Women entrepreneurship is the next women's movement. Women today are leaving the workplace in droves in favor of being at home, not as homemakers, but as job-making entrepreneurs. There are four main reasons why they are starting their own businesses.

1. **Flexibility**. Women want to have flexibility in their schedules so they can be there for their children's school

functions or if they need to take a day off because one of their children is sick.

2. **No income glass ceiling.** Women are seeking opportunities that will allow them to have an unlimited income potential. Salaries can be very limited in corporate America, especially for women.

3. **Dissatisfied with work environment.** Women are often seeking a work environment that is positive, supportive and encouraging. Many times this is hard to find when working for a corporation or business.

4. **Not challenged enough.** Being challenged in the workplace allows women to refine their skills and grow their confidence. Many organizations provide limited opportunity for women to fully utilize their skills and talents, leaving them feeling unfulfilled.

By starting their own business, women are able to create their desired lifestyle in an environment that allows them to have flexibility in their schedule, to put family and health first, to have unlimited earning potential, to create a positive and fulfilling work environment and to continually challenge themselves to grow personally and professionally.

Amazing Statistics
Female business owners will provide 5.5 million new jobs by 2018.

The Kauffman Foundation, one of the largest foundations in the U.S. and the world's largest devoted to entrepreneurship, has decided that this is the decade of the woman entrepreneur, a time for women to seek advisors, training and networking that will help them unleash their potential and fundamentally change their lives.

There is no doubt that this is a time of tremendous opportunity for entrepreneurs, especially women. I believe that for the first time in history, women can have a huge positive impact on our economy and provide solutions to social protection and education challenges for women and children.

In working with entrepreneurs for over two decades, I have found that most individuals who choose to follow their passion and/or choose the path to entrepreneurship have experienced a great sense of empowerment. Throughout their journey to success, these entrepreneurs encounter so many learning opportunities that lead to personal growth. Entrepreneurship allows individuals to tap into an amazing inner power that tremendously increases their self-worth and value. It is a great way to make a personal mark, leave a legacy behind and make a difference in the world.

Now Is Your Time

My purpose is to encourage you, to tell you that it's your time to take your rightful place as a strong, confident member of your family and society. It is time for you to have a healthy self-respect, a balanced self-love and a firm, unshakable confidence in your God-given gifts, talents and abilities. You have a destiny. Now's the time to realize who you really are and to act accordingly.

Challenge Time!

In this chapter you learned my Ignite Your Passion process. Now answer the following three questions mentioned earlier in this chapter:

1. What do I love to do?

2. What do I do that I can't help but do?

3. What do people tell me I'm good at or that I'm a natural at?

· ·

Empowering Quote:

"Without passion, you don't have energy; without energy, you have nothing. Nothing great in this world has been accomplished without passion."

—Donald Trump

· ·

Chapter 2

YOU HAVE TO
SEE IT TO BE IT

Change Your Mindset and Transform Your Life

The number one belief that holds people back is "I'm not ready."

Now is the time, to take charge of your future and start creating the life that you desire. What you see as possible determines your success. If you see an opportunity, then you are ready. It is important to always expand your possibilities, since possibilities create opportunity.

Ask yourself, "What is the opportunity I have in front of me now?"

Here are seven mindsets to adopt, so you can transform your life:

1. **Decide to take action.** Remember if you have the idea, you're ready. Make a plan and start taking consistent action toward your goals.

2. **Everything you experience is an opportunity** to learn or have a breakthrough.

3. **You must invest in yourself if you want others to invest in you.** This will build your confidence. What you learn will become yours for life. (We will be diving deeply into this topic in Chapter 6.)

4. **Fear and doubt only exist in your mind and are never the truth.** Have faith in your goals and focus on what really matters, which is how you can help others with your gift. It is not about you, it's about them.

5. **Creating systems will set you free.** (This topic will be addressed in Chapter 9.) When you are prepared, you will allow your creativity to work for you.

6. **Invest in a coach or mentor.** If you want to remove the guesswork and a lot of the struggles, hire someone who can show you how to get from where you are to where you want to be. This will save you a lot of time and money in the end!

7. **Be present to the opportunities in front of you and use your intuition to guide you in the right direction.**

All you have to do is ask yourself the following two questions: "Will this take me closer to my goals or away from my goals?" and "Is this decision in alignment with my values?"

Visualize Your Dreams

Visualization is a powerful tool to assist you in reaching your goals. The definition of visualization, according to Merriam Webster's Dictionary, is "the formation of mental visual images."

It was Wallace Wattles who first introduced the use of creative visualization. Wattles is best known for his book *The Science of Getting Rich,* published in 1910. His work clearly had a major influence on later self-help authors such as Napoleon Hill. And *The Science of Getting Rich* was itself a direct inspiration for the very popular book and movie *The Secret.*

It all comes down to our thoughts . . . our thoughts of what is possible.

This section is geared toward the ladies . . .

Have you ever heard this: "Women have to work a lot harder than men do." At the end of the day, it's not about equal rights, it's about how we think. We have to reshape how we view ourselves and realize our value. Or this: "The blunt truth is that men still run the world." In addition to external barriers erected by society, women are hindered by barriers that exist within themselves. We hold ourselves back in so many ways both big and small by lacking self-confidence or simply not believing in ourselves. Or have you ever heard this: "I will be happy if I just lose some weight." The truth is you have to be happy first in order to change your health or your body. We will never be perfect!

You must love yourself as you are and recognize your God-given talents and strengths and your unique characteristics. The most important part of reaching any goal is your perception of yourself. Do you want to be a famous speaker? Lead a successful business? Feel great about your body? Then, see yourself achieving it! "See it to be it" is what athletes say to visualize success. Live on your terms, no one else's. Create a new, empowered version of yourself.

Here are six tips to help you visualize success:

1. **Read inspiring books and stories**. Read about others who have achieved success in the area that you're interested in. This will allow you to believe that it's possible.

2. **Create a vision board**. Put together pictures and affirmations of what you want for yourself and your family and what you want your lifestyle to look like.

3. **Meditate daily**. This a great way to set your intentions for the day. Sit in a quiet place, take some deep breaths and focus on getting into a peaceful state. (I focus on the things that I'm grateful for, such as my family, my friends, my health and the opportunity to serve others with my gift.) This helps to remove what I like to call the "monkey chatter" going on in my mind. Then, visualize what you want for yourself or how you want your day to go. Be very specific. This is so powerful!

The universe will open up and create opportunities that will help you reach your goals.

4. **Journal daily**. Each day write down thoughts, words or phrases to describe what you want to achieve in your life or business. Or if you're more visual like me, you can use mind mapping with pictures to convey your thoughts. Be sure to write down the value you offer and what unique gifts and skills you possess that will allow you to succeed.

5. **Hang around other successful and positive people**. Start making time to connect with other like-minded individuals, especially in the area where you are wanting to succeed. You can learn a ton! You can even hire a coach or mentor, as I mentioned earlier in the chapter. That person can show you the way and eliminate some of the guesswork, avoiding timely and costly mistakes. Your coach or mentor will be your biggest cheerleader!

6. **Just start taking action**. Start taking action. Start moving in the direction of your goals. Just taking that action will motivate you to continue to move forward. Set obtainable goals for yourself, and in reaching them, you will gain more and more confidence along the way!

Challenge Time!

Your challenge #1: Pick at least three of the visualization activities above to focus on this week. Eventually you can add all six!

1. _____

2. _____

3. _____

Your Challenge #2: Create a Vision Statement

Write down your thoughts and ideas of what your business will look like a year from now. Be as specific as you can! (Make sure you do this for your first-year, third-year and five-year vision.)

My vision for my business is . . .

· ·

Empowering Quote:

"To accomplish great things we must first dream, then visualize, then plan . . . believe . . . act!"

—Alfred Montapert

· ·

Chapter 3

CREATE A NEW MONEY MINDSET FOR WHAT'S POSSIBLE IN YOUR BUSINESS

A re you sick and tired of being stressed out about money, how you're going to pay the bills, or how you will live your dream? Well the truth of the matter is, you can't change your life or business if you're worried about money, and you can't be happy, either, if you're constantly stressed about it. Chances are that you have something to share that offers a transformation or that can help people. If you're worried about or conflicted around money, you won't be able to get your gifts or talents out into the world. This chapter dives in deep to uncover where this *fear* around money comes from and how you can remove it from your world once and for all!

Not Charging What Your Worth
Comes from Old Negative Beliefs

Many small business owners struggle with not being able to charge what they're worth due to having an unhealthy relationship with money. This often comes from old negative beliefs about money that were most likely developed at an early age. These could have been adopted from how your parents talked about or treated money. For example, you may have heard these phrases when you were growing up: "Money doesn't grow on trees," or "You have to work hard for your money." These phrases demonstrate a belief in lack or scarcity around money.

You may also have formed negative beliefs around money due to a past difficult personal experience involving money or finances. If you are or have been in debt or you've struggled to pay your bills, these situations can also create a feeling of scarcity or the fear of not having enough money.

Either way, these negative beliefs around money are creating barriers and preventing you from reaching your true potential. They actually become self-sabotagers—jeopardizing any possible financial success you may have in your business.

My Personal Experience with Limiting Beliefs

I experienced some limiting beliefs when I was young. Money was pretty tight for my family and me when I was growing up. Although we lived in a middle class neighborhood, my parents had many children and animals to care for. There were five girls in my family, and we had a small farm in a suburb of Cleveland, Ohio. At one point we had five horses, a goat, five dogs, about thirty cats (yes, I said thirty cats—they kept multiplying!), three rabbits, two guinea pigs and two hamsters. My mom and dad both worked very hard for a local factory and each made a respectable income, but it didn't go very far considering the cost to take care of our family and the small zoo! Most of my childhood, I felt the financial strain our family was under. We weren't able to do a lot of things that most other families did: go on family vacations, go out to eat as a family or send us kids to a summer camp. Don't get me wrong, I can't really complain—I had a wonderful childhood with great memories; however, I do remember the feeling of lack when it came to money.

Also, there was a time in my life that I hit an all-time low financially and lost almost everything I owned. Nine years ago, I was running my business and doing very well with it. I was in a terrible relationship with a man who mentally abused me on a daily basis. This really affected my spirit and my motivation to work. I couldn't focus on my daily activities. As a solo-preneur, if I wasn't bringing in the money, the money wasn't coming in. So over a period of six months or so, things went south very fast. I had to make difficult decisions that would require making major changes in my life. I first got rid of the guy (definitely one of the best decisions I've ever made!), then I had to downsize my home and my car, sell my boat . . . the list goes on. Needless to say, it was a very humbling experience and a huge wake-up call. I remember feeling overwhelmed, frustrated and scared—how was I going to take care of myself and my son? As soon as I realized that these feelings were not serving me, I began to make a plan to change my circumstances. As soon as I started working the plan, I began gaining more confidence and started to turn things around.

Through my own experiences and the knowledge I have gained while working with my clients over the last twenty years, I have discovered the five keys to an empowered relationship with money.

Five Keys to Creating an Empowered Relationship with Money

In order to be financially successful, it is necessary for you to adopt a new money mindset. This means removing blocks and creating a new healthy relationship with money.

Oprah Winfrey once said, "If you want your life to be more rewarding, you have to change the way you think."

Key #1: Eliminate Old Beliefs That Are Sabotaging Your Business Success

As I mentioned earlier in this chapter, we often develop limiting beliefs around money, either from our relatives or through our personal life experiences. Either way, these limiting beliefs are very disempowering and will sabotage your success. You want to replace beliefs that are hindering your development with positive ones that will help you. There are four steps in eliminating these old beliefs. (These are Steps 1 and 2 of the **Passion Belief Method: Step 1, "Recognize Any Self-Sabotaging Beliefs," and Step 2, "Let Go."**)

1. **Recognize your old beliefs.** You can do this by thinking about your current financial situation. Do you detect any fear or scarcity when you think about money? Ask yourself, "What am I afraid of?" What are the feelings that come up? There are five primary underlying needs that we form our beliefs around. These needs are what drives you and others. These are the need for love, security, respect, to be valued and power.

2. **Acknowledge where these beliefs come from.** Ask yourself which of the primary underlying needs listed above you are attempting to satisfy with each belief. Where did the belief originate from or from whom did you adopt it?

3. **Forgive yourself and anyone else who was responsible for this old belief.** Forgiveness is an incredibly powerful tool. This is the biggest gift you can give yourself or others. It is also necessary so you can move on. Forgiving doesn't mean that you necessarily agree with the individual that you had the conflict with; it just means that you understand that that person had a positive intention for doing what he or she did, even though it does not currently serve you. You also must forgive yourself and take responsibility for the fact that you are where you are in your life and your business because of your beliefs and choices up until now. The great news is that you also have the opportunity to make different choices, coming from a new, empowered mindset.

4. **Let it go.** By holding on to these old beliefs, you will stay in a stuck pattern and continue to struggle and not get the results you desire. By letting go of them, you can create the space for new, empowering beliefs to develop and for opportunities to show up that will assist you in reaching your personal and financial goals. Take a deep breath and focus on the feelings that arise when you think about your current financial situation. Then, ask yourself the next three very simple questions. "Can I let it go? Will I let it go? When?" You can repeat this process until your current situation feels lighter and lighter and ultimately dissolves.

Many individuals have negative thoughts or beliefs about themselves. This process can be used for any limiting belief or doubt that you may have about yourself.

Below are the seven most common negative beliefs:

1. I can't do it.
2. I am not good enough.
3. I am not worth it.
4. I am alone.
5. What if . . . (usually relates to a fear of seeing a negative outcome)
6. I have no direction in my life.
7. I'm afraid.

Another old, limited belief I experienced growing up was that I should be conservative and play small. I was always an entrepreneur at heart—forever following my passions, which meant at an early age moving from job to job or opportunity to opportunity. This did not sit well with my dad. He always believed that you should find a solid company to work for, put your time in so that you could retire and then live off your Social Security and pension. (Unfortunately, that plan didn't work out so well for him, due to our ever changing government. But that's a separate conversation.) So I remember all of the times when I was getting closer and closer to discovering what I was most passionate about, and my dad would become very worried about my future, which caused part of me to feel like I was letting him down. Apparently, we had a different mindset in this area.

Key #2: Move Into Expansion Around Money

Depending on old beliefs or past experiences, individuals either feel contraction or expansion when it comes to making and managing money. Let's take a closer look at what this means.

Contraction = Feelings of Fear, Stress or Frustration
Expansion = Feelings of Joy, Abundance and Peace

You may feel contraction if you are experiencing financial challenges, such as trouble paying the bills or carrying a substantial amount of debt. These two situations can certainly cause you to have feelings of stress, fear or frustration. The problem is that these feelings can paralyze you, preventing you from taking positive steps in resolving your financial situation.

The great news is, once you develop a plan to either make more money or to pay off your debt, you can start moving into expansion. The beauty of it is that you don't have to be debt-free or financially successful to start feeling expansion; all you have to do is start working your plan.

Other examples of contraction:

- **Avoiding paying your bills.** Do you ever find yourself putting off or avoiding paying the bills? Quite often, it is not about paying the bills; it is about your limiting beliefs showing up (thoughts of lack and scarcity around money), or your resistance around money, or you playing small because you're shrinking in fear. These are the culprits preventing you from paying your bills.

- **Not having enough money in the bank.** When you don't have enough money in the bank to pay the bills, you may find that you're judging yourself or beating yourself up about it. Instead, create a plan and start paying off what you can each month until you get back on track again.

- **Owing someone money that results in avoiding that person because you are ashamed or embarrassed.** It can be extremely uncomfortable if you owe a friend or a family member money. Even if you have every intention of paying the person back as quickly as possible, you may be struggling just to get by, making it seem impossible to repay him or her. This can cause you to feel ashamed or embarrassed to even talk to the person. I suggest that you have a conversation with whoever lent you the money, let that person know that you still intend to pay it back, and commit to a plan to do so, even if it's just $100 a month until it's paid off. Most likely the person will understand what you're going through and accept those or similar terms. This may just restore your relationship.

- **When a client owes you money.** A client owing you money is an example of you giving your power away and letting your client take advantage of you. In your business, it is necessary to have defined boundaries set up from the get-go with your clients—for example, when they are expected to pay and what the consequences will be if they don't do so within that specific time frame, whether the consequences are late fees or termination of services. Stand in your power!

- **No savings in the bank.** If you have no money in savings, this is often related to your not feeling that you deserve to be wealthy or due to your being stuck in the cycle of lack and scarcity. A simple step you can take to change this is to make a point to start saving a portion of your income each month, even if it's only 5 percent. This can really allow you to start feeling more in control and confident in your ability to generate or manifest money in your life. You can slowly start increasing the amount you save each month. You'll be amazed at how quickly your savings account will start growing once you make the commitment to start saving. If your having no money in your savings account is due to the feeling that you don't deserve it, you'll need to address this by implementing the exercise introduced in Key #1, "Eliminate Old Beliefs" (on page [22]).

I love this quote by financial expert Suze Orman: "You can never solve a financial problem with money. The only way for you to have a larger net worth is for you to go within to see why you are going without."

Key # 3: Money Is an Exchange for Service

Many individuals, especially women, struggle when it comes time to ask for the sale, or they don't charge the rates they're worth. There comes a time to decide if you have a hobby or a business. A business makes money; if you're not making money, then you have a hobby. When it comes time to ask for the sale, many women have their old negative beliefs show up, feelings of "Am I good enough?" or "Is my product or service worth it?" If you are 100 percent sure that your product or service offers a solution to a problem that your target client is experiencing, then your product or service provides value and can truly help that client. By making your offer, you are offering a solution, providing value and remaining in integrity with yourself. So in essence, if someone pays you for your product or service, the money is an exchange for the service. Or you can even think of it as a reward for your service.

It's so amazing to me how many entrepreneurs feel so guilty making money, as if it's a bad thing. They say things like "I'm not doing it for the money." It really is OK to make money—even a lot of money. All it takes is a simple mindset shift. Think of it like this: the more money you make, the more people you've helped. Come from a place of serving, not selling.

Key #4: Start Focusing on Money

You may have heard this saying before: what you focus on you bring about. I can't stress enough how true this statement is. The problem is that when individuals are in debt, they focus on the debt. That will only keep you in debt. The only way to shift this is to start focusing on the solution and how you will start making more money.

Cash flow is one of the most important ingredients in business. If it's not in yours, it should be! There are three things to focus on when it comes to cash flow in your business.

1. **Tracking your money.** It is important to track your money daily. What money is coming in and what money is going out? Even if the number is zero or negative, do it anyway. You may initially get totally bummed if you have a "big ole zero" for the day, but use that energy to motivate you to make more money the next day. The importance of tracking is to learn

that you are in control of your money. Until you are in control, nothing can change!

2. **Investing.** Once you know how much money is coming in or not coming in, then you can assess what changes need to take place in your business. This is where you'll want to invest in it. This can mean, for example, bringing a business coach, a virtual assistant (an assistant that works remotely) or a marketing expert onto your team. Whatever area you're struggling in most is a great place to start. The more money you invest in yourself or your business, the more money you will make. Until you do this, you will continue to get the same dismal results.

3. **Make money.** Making money comes from marketing efforts and closing sales. As a business owner, you should focus on the income-producing activities that are going to bring more sales to your business, which means more cash flow.

It's also incredibly important to respect your money. Money is energy. You worked hard to earn it, so treat it with respect. For example, instead of leaving your change lying around in a sock drawer or in the cup holders in your car, take it to the bank and exchange it for dollar bills. Also, be sure to keep your money in a wallet that is organized and clean. Show your money some appreciation! Remember, what you focus on you bring about. So if you focus on money, you'll have more of it show up in your life.

It's also very important to have some goals set related to your finances. In the terrific book *The Slight Edge* the author, Jeff Olson, shares four Simple Strategies to assist you in setting your financial goals:

- List your specific and vivid dreams for your finances. Make sure to include a timeline.
- Write out the price you'll need to pay to achieve your goal.
- Outline your plan for getting started.
- Write down one simple daily discipline that you can incorporate into your life to help you reach that goal.

Key #5: Adopt a Healthy, Empowered Relationship with Money

There is nothing unspiritual about focusing on money. Money makes you more of who you are. For example, if you are a loving, caring and generous person, you'll be able to express that even more by having more money in your life, because you'll be able to help others in a bigger way. Once you own your value and start charging what you're worth, and you start making the money you deserve, everything will begin to shift. As a successful entrepreneur, you will grow in more ways than you ever thought possible. You will continue to build your self-worth and value more and more, and become more and more fulfilled. You will create a new, empowering belief system and stand in your power when it comes to money. This requires you to tap into your inner power, be your best self, be true to who you are and trust your abilities.

New "empowering" money mindsets:

- *Making more money means I provide more value to the world.* Since money is an exchange for the services you provide, the more money you make, the more people you've been able to help.
- *More money allows me to be more generous.* If you are a caring and generous individual, think of all the ways you could assist others or give back to your community if you made a substantial amount of money.
- *The more money I make, the more I can circulate it.* When you are consistently making money, on a monthly basis, in your business, you can begin to hire team members to help you spread your message in a bigger and more efficient way. You'll be able to provide opportunity/jobs to people in need so they can support themselves and their families.
- *I can become a great role model for what is possible.* By being successful in your business, you are demonstrating what is possible for other individuals who are aspiring to follow their passion and start their own business and/or make an impact by sharing their gifts with the world.
- *I can give back in a bigger way.* Start a charity or a foundation. Once you've built a successful and sustainable business, you now have the ability to take

a portion of your income and invest in a charity or a foundation. Whether it's supporting an existing cause that you are passionate about or starting your own foundation, there is nothing more rewarding than being a part of something bigger than yourself and using your resources to make a huge impact in your community or the world.

A Personal Experience in Circulating My Money

One of the scariest yet most fulfilling decisions I made in my business was when I was able to bring on my first team member. When I hired my first personal assistant / client relations manager, it was difficult to let go of control and trust in someone to represent my mission. However, it was so rewarding to know that I could help her generate an income, thereby helping her to support her family. When you have others assisting you and supporting you on your mission, you free up your time to start focusing on the things that you are most passionate about, and that can take your business to the next level.

Your New Powerful Mindset

With a new empowering and healthy relationship with money, you can move forward confidently when making financial decisions in your life and business. This will allow you to reach your personal and business financial goals so you can start living a life without limits. I encourage you to continue using the tools provided in this chapter to help you get through any barriers or roadblocks you may come across.

Challenge Time!

Answer the following questions:

1. Which of the seven negative belief statements listed on page 24 do you regularly experience? (List your top three.)

    _____

    _____

    _____

2. Choose one of the negative beliefs you listed in Question 1. Go through the letting go process included in Key #1, "Eliminate Old Beliefs"(on page 24). You may have to do this several times. Write down what your experience was like.

    _____

    _____

    _____

Empowering Quote:

"Once your mindset changes, everything on the outside will change along with it."

—**Steve Maraboli**

Chapter 4

BREAKING THROUGH RESISTANCE

Many of us are struggling, spending a great deal of time swimming upstream, rather than allowing our life to flow where we want it to go. What if you didn't have to struggle to get what you want? What if we can use the natural flow of life to support us in having what we desire? Think about a time in your life when you experienced being in a state of flow, or think of a day when everything seemed to go perfectly. You seemed to be in the right place at the right time. Then think of an average day. Which would you like to have? The greatest obstacle to being in the flow all of the time is resistance to what is.

Great news—you can let go of resistance just like you can let go of any other feeling. Resistance prevents us from moving ahead in all areas of our life.

So What Is Resistance Anyway?

Have you ever started a project, really giving it your all, and lost enthusiasm somewhere in the middle? That's resistance. Resistance can be very inconspicuous, but it's one of the main things that stops us from having, doing and being what we want in life. As a matter of fact, we often resist the things in life that we really like and care about. And if someone tells us to do something that is a surefire way to trigger resistance.

Resistance can be self-sabotaging and counterproductive, and it appears constantly, because we live in a world of "shoulds" and "have to's" and "must do's." This stirs up resistance. Anytime you are told you *should* do something or you *have to* do something, how do you feel inside? "No way! Don't tell me what to do!" That's just the nature of how the human mind works. We simply do not like being told what to do. Yet we are constantly "shoulding" on ourselves and wondering why we are not getting things done or having fun.

Here are some definitions of resistance that may help you recognize it:

- Resistance feels like you are trying to move forward with the brakes on
- Anytime you feel like you have to, must, or should do anything, you're in resistance.
- Resistance is pushing against the world, so it will push back.
- The feeling or thought "I can't" is resistance. It takes a conscious effort (habit) of holding down feelings; that unconscious habit is resistance.
- Resistance is when you haven't yet decided whether to do something or not, but you do it anyway and it's difficult. To make it easier, you must decide more definitely to do it or not to do it.

You can release resistance in this three step process:

1. Allow yourself to welcome the resistance in this moment.
2. Ask yourself one of the following three questions: Could I let go of this resistance? *or* Could I allow myself to feel this resistance in the moment? *or* Could I welcome the feelings of resistance? Then ask: Would I? When?
3. Repeat the above steps until you feel free.

Once you truly understand that you can let resistance go, you'll find yourself doing so without thinking about it very much. Release resistance anytime that you feel stuck.

Three Important Tips to Avoid Resistance

Ask, don't tell. Based on what was mentioned earlier, avoid bringing up unnecessary resistance in others by asking them to do something rather than telling them.

Do what you're doing and don't worry about what you're not doing. Very often, we feel that we should be doing something differently from the way we're doing it or that we should be doing something we're not doing. Remove the "shoulding" on yourself by allowing yourself to do what you're doing when you're doing it and stop thinking that you should be doing something else. Anytime you find yourself "shoulding," take time to release it.

Ease off the pressure. Does what you're doing feel hard? This is a clear sign that you've hit a wall of your own resistance. You are probably pressuring yourself or feeling pressure from someone else. If you are pressuring yourself, make a conscious effort to take the pressure off. As a result, you'll often find yourself getting more done, more quickly and easily. Here's an interesting fact: You can't feel others pushing you. You can only feel yourself pushing back. So if it seems that others are pressuring you, let go of your feelings of wanting to push back or resisting their pushes. As a result, you'll find that whatever you're doing will be done with much more ease and grace.

As you let go of your resistance in these areas, begin noticing the ease and flow that's always there, as well as the increased ease and flow that shows up as you let go of resistance. The more you practice letting go of resistance, the better you'll feel and the easier life will become.

When you are feeling stuck, it's a great time to get connected with your "why" again. Why are you doing what you're doing in the first place? This will typically give you the drive and energy you need to push forward. (We'll talk more about your why in Chapter 15.)

Resistance can be a major obstacle to having what you want and feeling the way you want to feel. However, you can easily let it go and enjoy the benefits of experiencing ease, grace and flow.

Challenge Time!

Answer the questions below.

1. What type of resistance shows up for you regularly?

2. How does it make you feel?

3. Use the three-step process explained in this chapter to release/dissolve these feelings. You may have to repeat the process several times for it to become lighter and lighter.

4. How do you feel now?

. . . .

Empowering Quote:

"Rise to the challenge of bringing your dreams to life! Do not be discouraged by resistance, be nourished by it. Success is the experience of rising to the level of your true greatness."

—Steve Maraboli

. . . .

Chapter 5

INCREASE YOUR NET WORTH BY INCREASING YOUR SELF-WORTH

There seems to be much confusion around the difference between self-esteem and self-worth. What is self-worth anyway? When you hear the word "self-worth," do you immediately think it's just another name for self-esteem? I think most people think the terms are synonymous. These two words are not the same. Self-worth is not self-esteem.

Before defining self-worth, let's take a look at self-esteem. The World Book Dictionary, a Thorndike-Barnhart dictionary, defines self-esteem as "thinking well of oneself; self-respect."

The concept or idea of someone having self-esteem was first conceived in the year 1657. It wasn't until 308 years later, 1965, that self-worth was recognized as a separate concept. Even today, many dictionaries still define self-worth as self-esteem.

Esteem is a high regard or favorable opinion for someone or something. It is based on something that someone has actually done, something external. To experience self-esteem you must be in the present.

For example: You may receive esteem based on your ability to do something well or your performance. This comes from a view of what others think about you.

So what is self-worth?

The World Book Dictionary defines self-worth as "a favorable estimate or opinion of oneself; self-esteem." The dictionary recognizes the distinction in concept but not entirely in meaning. You can view self-worth as a measure of your ability by your spirit or true self, your belief in yourself, what you believe yourself to be capable of. Self-worth comes from a source *inside* of us. We create it through faith and by acting on the sole belief that we matter. Self-worth is the foundation of our ability to believe in ourselves and value what we possess.

Self-worth is the portal through which self-esteem is received.

Self-esteem and self-worth are vital beliefs for empowering oneself. A valid sense of self-worth is necessary in order to attain peace, love, joy and power. Without self-worth, doubts and fears will persist until they invalidate our dreams and vision, and undermine our greatest accomplishments.

Now that we have clarified the meaning of self-worth, we can discover how it can significantly impact your net worth.

What Is Net Worth?

According to Investopedia.com, net worth is the amount by which assets exceed liabilities. Net worth is a concept applicable to individuals and businesses as a key measure of how much an entity is worth.

As Jim Rohn brilliantly stated, "Your net worth will likely never outperform your self-worth."

Five Simple Steps to Boost Your Self-Worth and Your Net Worth

1. **Ask yourself: What is your relationship with yourself?** How do you treat yourself? How do others treat you? Having a healthy relationship with yourself improves your relationship with others. A great example of this is when on an airplane they tell you to put your oxygen mask on first before you put one on anyone else. I have learned through my personal experiences, as well as those of my clients, that if we are not connected and emotionally available to ourselves, we cannot be connected and emotionally available to others.

   So what does a healthy self-relationship look like? A healthy self-relationship is the ability to value yourself as a person and accept and embrace your weaknesses. A great place to start cultivating a healthy relationship with yourself is by caring for your physical needs, including getting plenty of rest, eating a well-balanced, nutrient-rich diet and exercising daily. Second, focus on your inner world by regularly checking in with your emotions. Get connected with your spiritual self. Focus on joy by prioritizing activities that make you happy. What feeds your mind, body and spirit? Third, operate from integrity and stay true to your values and what is most important to you. Most often, how you treat yourself is how others will treat you.

2. **Decide to play big.** If you're playing small, then you are not serving the world with your gifts. Sometimes we shrink to fit, so we don't stand out or because we are afraid that if we put ourselves out there we may fail. Another reason is, we don't feel that we deserve success. In this case, there is often baggage that we're punishing ourselves for. Whatever it may be, acknowledge it, release it and forgive yourself. (Use the letting go process found in Chapter 3.) You cannot make a change unless you're willing to get real with yourself. It's time to declare your independence and go after what you want. You deserve it!

3. **Create a clear vision of what you want.** We talked about this in Chapter 2. In order to create a thriving, profitable business that you love, it is crucial to get clear on exactly what you want your life and business to look

like. Visualize your ideal day doing what you want to be doing, with the people you want to work with and with you best serving your customers or clients with your specific products and services. You can actually create the business of your dreams, on your terms—it's really up to you!

4. **Decide who you will become to fulfill your vision.** In order to reach your true potential, you must become the best version of yourself. Are there any areas that you need to develop or grow in for you to be able to reach your goals? You may have heard of the popular saying by Tony Robbins "If you're not growing, you're dying." This may sound harsh, but if you compare it to a plant or more specifically a fruit, it makes perfect sense. For instance, let's look at an apple. When an apple is still on the tree, it's growing. But once it's picked, it starts to die. This isn't necessarily apparent. When you see an apple at the grocery store, you don't think of it as something that's dying. In fact, you probably think the opposite, which is that the apple is ripe and at its ideal state. However, this isn't true. As a person you are not any different from that apple. Things may look great on the outside—fancy cars, big house, high salary etc.—but in many cases we are dying on the inside. Rotting when we appear ripe—a life where you're unhappy, unfulfilled and unsatisfied; a life without meaning. What changes will you have to make to

reclaim your life, be of service to others and live a life full of passion?

Practice expecting the best. Be the person you strive to be and your brain will follow.

5. **Do the impossible now.** In order to achieve a high level of success in your life and/or business, you must push yourself beyond what you thought was possible. This requires getting uncomfortable and stepping outside your comfort zone on a regular basis. This is something that I practice consistently. If there is an idea that I have or an opportunity that comes my way that makes my heart beat fast, I know that it's something I have to do! That's when I've seen the biggest growth within myself. It is through those times that I stepped outside of my comfort zone. This is how you, too, can grow exponentially.

So, in summary, we have learned how your self-worth impacts your level of success in your life and business.

Beliefs=Feeling=Thoughts=Actions=Results

Just to clarify, we're not talking about self-worth and net worth being tied solely to how much money you have (money does not make you who you are). We're talking about how your concept of yourself calls the shots on the level of the income or success you're able to achieve. Your self-esteem and self-worth affect everything you have and do!

Challenge Time!

Ask yourself: What would I do to achieve my goals if fear and money weren't an issue?

Write down your thoughts:

_____

_____

_____

_____

· ·

Empowering Quote:

"When you adopt the viewpoint that there is nothing that exists that is not part of you, that there is no one who exists who is not part of you, that any judgment you make is self-judgment, that any criticism you level is self-criticism, you will wisely extend to yourself an unconditional love that will be the light of the world."

—Harry Palmer

· ·

Chapter 6

WHEN YOU INVEST
IN YOURSELF, OTHERS
WILL INVEST IN YOU

I nvesting in yourself is the best return on investment you can have. Whether it's growing your business, learning a new skill or working on your creativity or personal development, you need to give to yourself first, before you can give to others. So it's not always money that's required when you're investing in yourself. Time and energy are just as important. Investing in yourself requires learning how to maximize the unlimited potential that lies within your mind and body.

Why Is Investing in Yourself So Powerful?

Investing in yourself sends a powerful message to yourself and the world. The message is:

The value and potential that I possess is important enough to me that I'm going to give it the energy, space and time to grow and create results.

If we don't spend our energy, time and money developing ourselves, we will start becoming smaller. If you don't value yourself, you will exhaust yourself looking for others to give this to you. If you don't speak up for yourself, you will eventually become frustrated and bitter inside. If you don't trust your intuition, the signals will become weaker and you may lose the effectiveness of this source altogether. If you neglect your creativity, you will struggle the next time you need a new idea.

When you invest in yourself, especially in business, opportunities will present themselves to support your moving forward. This has happened to me countless times, and I've experienced it firsthand with many of my clients.

I'd like to share a poignant story about one of my clients that shows just how powerful investing in yourself can be.

One day I met with a potential new client named Lisa at a local Starbucks. Lisa had been referred to me by a friend of mine. She was a very talented, yet struggling, interior designer.

She was also feeling somewhat depressed and not very inspired. She explained to me that one of her goals was to get to a point where she could wake up in the morning and actually feel excited about the day. Lisa's world revolved around taking care of her husband and children, and she didn't do much for herself, but she had been doing quite a bit of interior design work for some friends and family. They absolutely loved her work and continually praised her and told her how talented she was. The problem was that nobody ever offered to pay her, and she was afraid to ask them to pay her. Over time, this led to Lisa becoming quite frustrated and even resentful. I told Lisa that I could help her, and that one of my specialties was helping individuals own their value so they could get paid what they're worth.

I offered Lisa one of my coaching programs that would assist her in building a successful business that she could be passionate about. I remember there was a lot of fear coming up for her; she had never done anything like this for herself. She had never "invested in herself" like this before. But, regardless of the fear, she decided to move forward anyway. I remember her writing me a check right then and there for the coaching program.

I also remember getting a call from Lisa the very next day, in which she said, "Megan, you're never going to believe what happened a few hours after I met with you yesterday. I got a call from my friend [ironically, it was actually one of the friends who were taking advantage of her services], and she told me about an event she was asked to coordinate. She needed someone to be in charge of the decorations and she offered the job to me! The best part, it's is a paying job and the amount she offered to pay me just happened to be the exact same amount that I had just invested in your program!" How cool is that!

When you're willing to say yes to yourself and take that leap of faith, the universe will provide you with amazing rewards.

I would like to share some incredible ways that you can invest in yourself.

Megan's Top 10 Ways to Invest in Yourself

1. **Set goals.** Learn how to set personal and business goals for yourself. If you're not taking the time to set goals, it's like driving in the dark with the headlights turned off. You will not know where you're going and you will waste precious time. Be sure to also set some time frames in which to meet your goals. And they should be **SMART** goals –**S**pecific, **M**easurable, **A**ttainable, **R**elevant and **T**imely.

2. **Honor your intuition.** You can show yourself love by trusting your gut and honoring the message that it's sending. Listening to your intuition will allow you to make better decisions. Valuing your intuition, by not allowing the thoughts, feelings or statements of others to take away from what you know to be true, is very empowering. Paying attention to how you feel will help you to make better, smarter and quicker decisions. I know for me personally, if I choose to ignore my gut or intuition when I feel a strong feeling about something,

it almost always is a decision or action that I end up regretting. I have learned to always trust my intuition, and that is what leads me in my life and business.

3. **Invest time in your creativity.** Our creativity doesn't have to diminish after childhood. In fact, it is believed that the peak of creativity in most people is around thirty to forty years old (Lindaur, 1998, Marisiske &Willis, 1998). Creativity can be the catalyst in the manifestation of continual learning and lifelong activity. Creating new ideas brings your life new energy. It allows us to be inspired, have fun and appreciate the beauty in the world.

4. **Invest in building your confidence.** People who know their value have something to say, and others will listen. You can invest in yourself by developing an understanding of the value that you possess and offer others. Learn to have the courage to speak your truth. The more you love yourself and own the value that you offer, the more confident you will become in sharing it with others.

5. **Read educational books.** Books or audiobooks are an awesome resource to build your knowledge and expertise in any area.

6. **Attend seminars and workshops to expand your knowledge and skills in your business and/or personal life.** This will also give you the opportunity to meet and interact with individuals who are like-minded.

7. **Take care of your health.** Eat right each day, fueling your body with nutrients. When you focus on eating organic and healthier choices, you will feel better and have more energy. I know that the unhealthy burger or cupcake gives us instant gratification, but if you're like me, you regret it later, because you feel lousy afterward. Exercise daily. Do something every day to get moving and get your heart rate up, even if it's just walking the dog. Exercise gives you the energy to take on the day with confidence because of how it makes you look and feel. I have dedicated a whole chapter to health (Chapter 12) because of just how important it is to your success!

8. **Choose to be happy.** Happiness is a choice. Happy people choose to focus on the positive aspects of life, rather than the negative. They are not held hostage by their circumstances. They look at all the reasons to be grateful. Abraham Lincoln once said, "Most people are about as happy as they make up their minds to be."

9. **Work on your bucket list.** Take time to start the creation of a bucket list. Your bucket list is meant to be a list of everything you want to achieve, do, see, feel and experience in your life. Your list may be ongoing, but you can start by writing one hundred things down. Then, each month or so, make sure you're knocking out at least one of the items on your list.

10. **Invest in a coach.** A coach can assist you in putting all of these strategies into action. A coach is your

partner in success. It is your coach's job to assist you in creating and implementing your success plan, so you can become the best that you can be.

When you invest in yourself, a world of opportunities will open up for you. If you have a business where you sell your services, you must know that no one will invest in you until you invest in yourself first.

Investing in yourself emotionally, physically, spiritually and financially will allow you to become the best version of yourself. When you are the best version of yourself, you will be an attraction magnet to others!

Challenge Time!

What are three ways from the list I provided that you will invest in yourself in the next thirty days?

1. _____.

2. _____

3. _____

. . . .

Empowering Quote:

"Investing in yourself is the best investment you will ever make. It will not only improve your life, it will improve the lives of all those around you."

—Robin Sharma

. . . .

Chapter 7

YOUR UNIQUE GIFT, YOUR PASSION, YOUR VALUE

Passion Belief Method Step 3, "Clarify Your Passion/Your Gift"

O ne day, I was in my daughter's theater classroom and I saw a sign on the wall that said, "Be Yourself—An original is always worth more than a copy." It got me thinking about many of the people that I come across in business, and some of my clients when I first started working

57

with them. They look at what other people are doing in business and attempt to copy them. I personally believe that is the kiss of death for your business and most often your happiness. Each of us is unique. We have our own set of God-given talents, skills, education and experiences. When you start getting clear on what your gifts are and what you're passionate about—this is when the magic happens—this is when you can discover your brilliance. When you create a business around your gifts/passion, you will not only be passionate about what you do, but your ideal clients will be attracted to you—the people you are meant to serve.

If you're not clear on what your unique gift or passion is, I have three ways to help you identify it.

1. Your unique gift/passion is something that you can't help but do, something that comes naturally.
2. People will often comment on or compliment you on it.
3. This is something you absolutely love!

Maya Angelou once said, "You can only become truly accomplished at something you love. Don't make money your goal. Instead, pursue the things you love doing, and then do them so well, that people can't take their eyes off of you."

Sometimes our gifts come so naturally to us that we don't even realize how special they are. When you are able to share your gift, it allows you to live your purpose.

It is important to use your gift regularly in order to develop it. As you use it, you will discover ways that you can perfect it.

One of the most common challenges that entrepreneurs or business professionals face is not being able to understand the value of what they offer. So many well-intentioned professionals are giving their time, gifts and talents away. Think where this may be showing up for you.

Examples of giving your time, gifts and talents away:

1. **Overdelivering.** This is especially common with coaches and consultants; they often spend too much time in their sessions or feel the need to jam-pack everything that they know into the session, leaving the client confused and exhausted.

2. **Volunteering too much.** Many of us have a problem saying no, so we overextend ourselves and commit to volunteering at this event or that event, serving on multiple boards or committees, leaving us no time to focus on our work or our family.

3. **Not charging enough for your services.** Many business owners are undervaluing their services and pricing their products and services way too low.

4. **Not regularly increasing your prices.** Your prices should be increased on a regular basis. Typically, each year is a good rule of thumb.

5. **Not asking for a raise.** Many employees are not offered and don't ask for a yearly raise.

These situations all come from having a low self-worth and not knowing your unique value and the gifts you have to share with the world.

When referring to value, I am referring to the following definition of the word: "regard that something is held to deserve; the importance, worth or usefulness of something."

Your value is made up of many things: your unique God-given talents, your skills, your education and your experiences. As you can see, there is no one else like you; it's virtually impossible. (I have an identical twin sister, and in many ways even we are completely different. For example, I love to speak in front of large groups where she does not; she says that the thought of it scares her. And she is a very skilled and passionate bookkeeper, and that is a skill I do not possess or have any interest in.)

You are an amazingly unique individual. People will want to work with you because of who you are and what you bring to the table that is different from everyone else. That is why there is truly no such thing as competition, especially if you build your business based on your unique gifts/passion.

It's Time to Create a New Belief System and Stand in Your Power When It Comes to the Value That You Offer!

You want to have your prices for your programs and services reflect your value, so you can start earning what you're worth.

To give you an example: my gift is to help individuals remove blocks that are holding them back and realize their value, so they can reach their true potential.

I believe that we are all blessed with our own unique gifts and it is our responsibility to share them. When you operate from a space of tremendous service and you use your gifts to help others, you will change the world one person at a time.

Challenge Time!

Think about the gifts, talents and skills that you possess. Next, think about your career or business. Answer the following questions:

1.   What is the unique value that you offer?

2.   What problem does your product or service solve?

3.   What is the solution or transformation that you offer?

. . . .

Empowering Quote:

"Strive not to be a success, but rather to be of value."

—Albert Einstein

. . . .

Chapter 8

OFFERING YOUR GIFT
BY SERVING NOT SELLING

A big challenge today, and something I've personally noticed while working with hundreds of entrepreneurs, is that many have a difficult time selling themselves and their products or services. Many times these same individuals were highly successful as employees in corporate America, and some were even "rock star" sales professionals.

I know I certainly used to have a challenge in this area, even though I've been in sales my whole life and even taught sales for years. When I was ready to present my first offer for my own business, I felt uneasy and didn't quite know the right words to say. I often wondered, "Why is this so hard?"

Well, there is actually a big difference when you're selling for yourself—especially when you're a passionate entrepreneur. We are all wanting to share our mission and our gifts and make a difference in the world. Our main focus isn't necessarily to make a sale on a product. We are marketing ourselves, which makes us a heck of a lot more vulnerable. We are afraid that our clients or customers may reject us. It's not as easy to detach ourselves from the outcome, as if we were selling someone else's products or services, as this is part of who we are.

In order to successfully price and sell our expertise, we must be courageous and present ourselves with confidence. There are six things that will allow you to do just that.

1. **Realize your value.** It's extremely important for you to understand the value of your products and/or services. As discussed in Chapter 7, knowing the unique value that you offer is key. Can your product or service truly help someone solve a problem or challenge? If so, then you are incredibly valuable!

2. **Identify your target market.** The more specific you are with identifying whom you want to serve and how you want to serve them, the more successful your business will be. It is also a lot easier to grow a business if you are focused on a specific target market. Many business owners are afraid to limit their target

market and feel that they can help everyone. Although that may be true, that is not the approach you want to take with your marketing. People hire a professional or an expert to help them solve a specific problem they are experiencing. They are looking for answers and solutions. They buy systems, processes or steps that are proven to work. They want something that has a beginning, middle and end and will assist them in getting the results they desire.

Example:

Instead of helping business owners build their business, you can assist small business owners in creating a unique personal brand. If you're still having trouble with narrowing your niche, think of who specifically you would like to work with and who you can best serve with your unique value.—That will help you get clear.

3. **Present your offer with confidence.** How can you describe the transformation you have to offer in a way that it will resonate with your ideal client? What are the words to say that will allow that client to know that you're the one who can take him or her from where the client is to where the client wants to be? It is important to understand that not everyone is your ideal client— the ones with whom your product or service resonates are the ones that you want to focus on.

4. **Solidify your signature system.** What is the system or the process that you use with your clients to get results?

How do you do what you do? Once you have identified each step, be sure you give your system a name and brand it. Also, it's important to decide how you can deliver your system. For example, you can deliver your system via an online training program, a workbook or a video or audio training series.

5. **Be prepared.** Put together a sixty-second introduction that allows you to share with others who you are, what your expertise is, your mission and with whom you aspire to work. Also, be sure to put together an irresistible offer (an invitation to work with you) to present to your ideal client, whether it's one-on-one, over the phone or from the stage. Make sure that you have various programs with various levels of investment. A great rule of thumb when pricing your programs is that the more one-on-one time the client gets with you, the bigger the investment!

Four elements of creating your irresistible offer:

- Your product offers a relevant solution to a problem that your audience is experiencing.
- It is delivered in a desirable way that is simple, convenient and easy to access.
- You offer a bonus or incentive to inspire clients to take action. Bonus ideas you can offer are: another program you can provide, your book, a video or audio training or even someone else's product or program.

- It has a limiter. For example, this offer is only good during this event (or for the next forty-eight hours), or this offer is only available for the first twenty people to sign up.

The key is to make your offer so irresistible that customers are inspired to take action right away. This does not mean dropping your price below its value. If the value is there and you present your offer with confidence, the right clients/customers will move forward.

6. **Use the S.E.R.V.E. sales success formula.**

Use this formula as your key to success in creating and delivering authentic and effective sales conversations, conversations that will inspire your ideal clients to say *yes* to working with you.

<u>S</u>hare. Have your prospect share the one thing that he or she would like to be different in life or business. Reveal the problem or challenge that the prospect is experiencing. (You can customize this based on the products or services you offer.)

Sample question: "What is the one thing you would like to change in your life/or business?"

<u>E</u>stablish the cost of continuing on the same path that the prospect is on. Reveal the pain points that he or she is experiencing. (This step is necessary to allow the potential client to get emotionally connected to the problem.)

Sample question: "If you continue on this same path, how do you think it will impact your relationships, your health, your finances, your goals/dreams?"

Results. What are the results that the prospect truly desires? What are his or her goals and dreams?

Sample question: "If you could paint a picture of the life/business [customize, based on your business] you desire, what would that look like for you? Be as specific as possible. (Example: What would your average day look like, who would you be working with, how much money would you be making and what would your lifestyle look like?) How would you feel when you . . . [repeat what the prospect shared]?"

Value. Provide value by sharing two tips or strategies that the potential customer can implement right away to move toward his or her goals. (This will allow the prospect to experience your work, your expertise. Be sure not to over deliver here!)

Extend your offer. Here is where (if it's a fit) you'll recommend a product or service that you offer that will provide the solution to the prospect's problem. This is the transformation that you offer.

Sample question: "I believe I have a clear understanding of where you are and where you want to be. Now I'd like to, with your permission—recommend what I feel would be the next best step for you to reach your goal of [fill in what the prospect shared]. Would you like to hear my recommendation?"

If the prospect answers yes, then you share the appropriate offer (your solution/your transformation).

After you share your offer, ask the prospect, "Would like to know the price?" Once you share the price, be silent . . . wait for a response.

Then say . . . "On a scale from one to ten, with one being absolutely <u>no</u> and ten **being absolutely <u>yes</u>, where do you stand** with your level of interest?"

Be silent.

If it is a ten, you say, "Great, so here's how we get started."

If it's below a ten, like a seven, eight or nine, ask the prospect, "What would it take to get you to a 10?" (Then, satisfy any objections or concerns the prospect may have.)

If it is a five or less, you can ask the prospect why. Chances are the product or service you offered is not the right fit for them.

Remember: you are not there to convince the prospect, you are there to get the potential client to a decision.

Bonus: If your prospect has an objection, that's great. It's not a no. It's a yes, but . . . This gives you the opportunity to provide more value to make sure the prospect is clear on why he or she should move forward with your offer!

Selling has changed dramatically over the last few years. Long gone are the days of selling the features and benefits of your products or services and wowing your customers so much that they buy from you. In the past, ego was a big part of the sales process, a more self-centered approach. Typically the more bold, confident and persuasive you were, the more successful you were in closing the deal. The rest of society became paralyzed with fear at the thought of selling.

Today, people are looking for solutions to their problems and a way to get their needs met. If we make it about us, they will often tune out and most likely be turned off.

That is why coming from a place of service versus selling works so well. You can connect with your clients from where they are and begin to earn their trust and respect by having a genuine and authentic conversation with them. And if your product or service offers a solution for them to get from where they are to where they want to be, there is a better than average chance that they will move forward in purchasing it.

Another important tool to have in your selling tool belt is the ability to establish the "cost of not doing anything" with your client. For instance . . . if your potential client is concerned about the investment, you can demonstrate to the client the cost of not doing anything to change the present situation. For example, the client obviously has some sort of challenge, issue or problem he or she is currently facing or the client most likely wouldn't be to talking to you in the first place. If the prospect poses a concern about pricing or cost, you can simply say, "Let me ask you this: if you continue on this same path, six to twelve months down the road there is a very good chance you will be in the same place if not worse off. The real question is . . . What is the cost of not doing anything about it? How will it affect your health, well-being, relationships and your finances?" This allows the client to go back to the pain and often gives him or her the final push required to take action.

Selling can be fun. It really is a way to offer solutions to problems and serve people in a powerful way. Think about it like this: if you don't offer your product or service, because you're afraid of being too pushy or afraid that you'll get rejected, you're robbing that person of a solution to his or her problem or a possible transformation in his or her life. Give your clients the power and the opportunity to make their own decision.

Challenge Time!

Answer the following questions, to assist you in getting clear on your specific target market and what problem you will solve with your business. Gaining clarity in these areas will allow you to become more effective during the sales process. We will start broad and narrow it down.

1. Who can benefit from your knowledge, product or service?

2. Out of all those people, who wants your product or service? (This is different from needing.)

3. Who is not only able but willing to pay for your services? (People buy based on emotions; remember to find out what their pain points are and what solution they're looking for.)

4. What are your prospects talking about with their friends, researching on the Internet and spending money on?

5. What benefits would they gain from purchasing your product or service?

6. What kind of client do **you** want? (Knowing the people you work best with will ensure that you do your best work—not only will it make you happy, but it will also feed the referral funnel.)

Typically your ideal client is someone like you. What type of people do you naturally find yourself drawn to?

· ·

Empowering Quote:

*"Anyone can be great,
because anyone can serve."*

—**Martin Luther King Jr.**

· ·

Chapter 9

CREATING AN ENVIRONMENT AND PLATFORM FOR SUCCESS— SYSTEMS WILL SET YOU FREE

Creating systems in your life and work will allow you to become more productive, effective and efficient. It will also help you to leverage your time. In this chapter, we're going to explore three main areas that require structure. Those areas are your physical environment, your business systems/processes and your daily routine.

Your Successful Physical Environment

When it comes to setting your business up for success, one of the key areas that is often forgotten is your physical office space. So that's where we're going to start. This space should be considered sacred! Your work area can improve your focus, your mood, your creativity, your productivity and your results!

I remember a few years ago, when I moved into my husband's house after we got engaged, there was no specific office space for me to set up my business. So I adopted the kids' craft room as my new workspace. This room was full of craft items and projects and was, quite frankly, a big mess! I set up my little work area in a corner of the room. My cat, Chloe, was also sharing the space with me. Her litter box was literally right next to my desk, and oh what a joy that was. I have to say it's very difficult to feel empowered and present yourself professionally when you are in a cluttered space and you have your cat doing her business during an important call!

I decided that things needed to change drastically. I told my husband that I was going to transform the craft room (that the kids rarely used) and turn it into my new office. After Chloe was relocated to the laundry room, I began to paint the walls a pale, sunny yellow. I added window treatments, artwork and even a small couch with colorful pillows. All of a sudden, my office became a cozy and cheery place to be. Now when I enter my office, I feel very energized and inspired and ready to work! I also use the space to conduct VIP days with my clients.

I have come up with three tips that you can utilize to design an office space that will inspire and motivate you as you're working toward success.

Have a dedicated room for your office. In order for you to be laser-focused with your clients or on your work, your environment should be quiet and private. Unless you are living alone, it's pretty unlikely that a corner of the room or a shared office space will provide you either. (Trust me, I know from experience!)

If you simply don't have a dedicated space in your home currently, a great idea would be to set up a room divider. This can create the professional atmosphere and privacy you need to maximize productivity.

Keep your workspace free from all clutter. Running a business creates a lot of paperwork. This paperwork can easily pile up and create clutter. Clutter blocks the free flow of energy and can cause a major distraction. Look around your office for dust, dirt, dead plants, old equipment, stacks of papers and any other items that you don't require for your work.

As soon as you can clean this clutter, you'll start creating the space for success. Set up storage and filing systems that work for you and keep things organized. You can even hire an organization expert, if you're organizationally challenged.

Surround yourself with things that inspire you. Be sure to display items that add visual stimulation and inspiration. For example: artwork, sculptures, awards, vision boards (boards where you display pictures of what you want to achieve), treasured mementos and even positive quotes. Be sure you don't create a different kind of clutter.

You can also add inspiration with plants, flowers, music and scented candles. The idea here is to create a desirable ambiance that makes you feel uplifted and joyful.

If you are experiencing stress, confusion or limited success in your business, it's time to change your environment. Use these tips as a guide.

Your office should inspire you to tap into your inner power, to create from and serve your higher self. It's so important to take the time to create the right environment that is going to lay the foundation for more satisfaction and success.

Your Successful Systems and Processes

Setting up systems for your business success is the next important area we're going to cover.

You must have a solid structure in place to be recognized as a professional business and a legitimate business owner. Also, this structure will allow you to consistently grow your business. Your potential clients and customers must have a way to connect with you and find out about what you do. After the initial connection, it is essential to also have a way for them to stay connected with you, so that you can start building a relationship with them. Having the proper business structure in place allows you to do that.

Seven Main Components to
Create Structure in Your Business

1. **Website.** This is a place where your visitors can get to know what you and your business are about and start getting a feel for who you are and what you stand for. It is a place where they can go and discover how you can assist them in getting what they want.

2. **Special offer.** Create a "free gift" to offer them value, such as a free report, a guide, a video or audio training, offering tips, strategies or how-tos or resources about their greatest needs, wants and interests.

3. **Opt-in form.** A place where your visitors can put in their name and email address, so they can receive your free offer.

4. **A way to collect names (build your list).** Once your visitors put their information into the opt-in form, their name will go on your list, allowing you to communicate with them regularly to nurture the relationship, continue to provide value, build trust and credibility and then eventually make an offer.

5. **A way to process sales.** It is necessary to have a shopping cart service and a merchant account in place, so that you are ready to process sales and accept payments online from your customers.

6. **Create high ticket packages.** Develop packages that deliver a big result and solve a specific urgent problem that your clients have. Doing this immediately shifts

you from chasing low-paying clients to being attractive to clients who are highly motivated and value the transformation you offer. These clients can pay you anywhere from $2,000 to $10,000 (or more) for your transformational program. The most incredible thing about this is that you only have to work with a small number of clients at this level to make a great income. No more trading time for dollars; now you can leverage your time and focus on value instead of dollars per hour.

7. **Develop a sales process.** This will allow you to easily turn your ideal prospects into paying customers. In Chapter 8, you learned my S.E.R.V.E. sales success formula, which is a surefire process to gain new clients.

Your Daily Routine for Success

Managing your time for maximum results can be a challenge for most.

Do you ever feel like you are running around ragged all day in a hundred different directions? Are you trying to juggle all of the duties of being a business owner, a spouse, a parent and a friend? Are you feeling pulled in so many different directions that you've lost sight of who you are and your initial vision of why you wanted to start your own business in the first place?

Many heart-felt entrepreneurs and business professionals struggle with managing their time on a daily basis, resulting in their not accomplishing what they set out to, leaving them feeling stressed and frustrated at the end of the day. The good news is, I have some great tips to help you gain more time and freedom in your business.

Here is the Wiki definition of time management: "the act or process of planning and exercising conscious control over the amount of time spent on specific activities, especially to increase effectiveness, efficiency and productivity."

Over the years, I've learned from many time management experts and through my own experiences in my own business career, and I want to share my Top 10 time management tips.

Megan's Top 10 Tips for Creating More Time
for Yourself and Becoming Ultraproductive

1. **Set up systems to support you.** As we mentioned earlier in this chapter, systems can set you free. Effective marketing and scheduling systems will allow your business to run efficiently and free up a ton of time.

2. **Focus on revenue-generating activities.** As a business owner, the main thing you should be focusing on is income-producing activities. In other words, focus on things that are, or will potentially be, making money. These things can include making opportunity calls (to potential clients or partners), conducting consulting calls or strategy sessions, follow-up calls and speaking engagements. After you get the previous items completed, then you can focus on your marketing and program planning, blogging and email follow-up.

3. **Delegate the stuff you don't have time to do or don't like to do.** There are so many tasks in a day-

to-day business that are time stealers, especially if you are not skilled to do them. Many things in your business can be delegated to an assistant, to another team member or outsourced altogether. If you do not have any team members, you may want to seriously consider hiring a virtual assistant (an assistant that can work remotely) to do things such as marketing, website updates, customer service calls, cold calling to potential prospects, etc. Bottom line is, you should be focusing on the things in your business that only you can do and that are going to directly impact the growth of your business. I know this is a scary step for most business owners. But you can do this. I'll tell you how and why it makes perfect sense.

Let's say that your time is worth $100 an hour; quite possibly it might be worth much more than that, but we'll just use this amount as an example for now. Let's also say that you're spending ten hours a week on administration tasks. If you paid yourself that $100 an hour for the time put in on the admin tasks, that would be $1,000 per week and $4,000 per month. Those tasks can be done by an assistant or virtual assistant that makes $20.00 per hour. So let's take that ten hours and multiply it by $20—that's $200 per week and $800 per month. If you took those ten hours per week (forty hours per month) and solely focused yourself on income-producing activities, how much money could you make in those hours? Would you be able to make more than the $800 per month needed to pay your assistant? Of course you would; in fact, I'm certain you would be able to grow your business exponentially. So the math makes sense.

If you're not moving forward on this, you must ask yourself: "What is holding me back?" Is it fear of not finding the right person? Is it having to let go of control? Or is it that you don't believe that you can bring in the money to cover the expense of an assistant? You will have to let go of those limiting beliefs and shift your thoughts to thoughts that are empowering and supportive of your business goals.

4. **Batch your time.** Schedule your time in different blocks, or "batch your time." For example, maybe on Mondays, Wednesdays and Thursdays from 9 to 11 a.m., you do your office work. Monday afternoons from 1 to 3 p.m. is your time to create new programs or marketing strategies. Tuesdays from 10 a.m. to 2 p.m., you write copy for your blog or newsletter. Wednesday and Thursday afternoons from 12 to 3 p.m., you meet with your clients. You get my point. When you have designated focused time for certain tasks, you can get so much more accomplished. I realize that sometimes you'll have to adjust your schedule for other things that come up, and that's OK. You can use this schedule as a strong guideline.

5. **Use tools to help you with scheduling or documenting dates or information.** There are so

many tools available to assist you in scheduling and managing your time. There's Google Calendar, Outlook, TimeTrade, or if you're like me you can use a good old-fashioned weekly planner. (This drives my very tech-savvy husband crazy!) I do also use TimeTrade as my online scheduler. I recommend having a dry erase board in your office that you can use to post dates for events and launches throughout the year. Another great tool is a handheld recorder to record your thoughts and ideas as necessary throughout the day. These tools can save you a lot of time.

6. **Use a family calendar.** If you have a family, I highly recommend having a family calendar, as well, that's integrated with your business. This way, you can put all of your family's activities right in your master calendar, so you don't miss a thing. You can at least attempt to plan business events or meetings around your priorities, at the top of which should always be your family.

7. **Designate workout and mediation time.** I think it's really important to have a consistent time set to work out and meditate each day (preferably in the morning, to start your day off right). Otherwise there's a good chance that you won't do it. Your health is the most important factor in your life; that is why I dedicated a whole chapter to this topic. (Chapter 12). Without your health nothing else matters. Working out will help to alleviate stress and provide you the energy you need to accomplish everything you have to do each

day. Meditation will help you to start your day with a positive mindset. Be sure to set your intentions for the day!

8. **Preplan your meals.** An area many women are challenged in is finding the time to prepare nutritious meals for their families and themselves. The best way to accomplish this is to plan your meals ahead of time. Saturday mornings over coffee, plan out all of the meals you would like to have throughout the week. Make your store list. Sunday afternoon, you can shop for the items you'll need. When you get home, you can cook your meats (chicken or steak) for the week, and anything else you can prepare ahead of time and refrigerate or freeze for later. (This is a great example of batching your time!) This way when you get home in the evening on a weekday, after running around all day, you can prepare a delicious meal in no time!

9. **Get plenty of sleep.** Make certain you attempt to get at least eight hours of sleep each night, so your body can rejuvenate itself, and you can wake up feeling fresh and ready to take on the day.

10. **Schedule downtime.** Every minute of your life should not be planned. Make sure you schedule downtime for you and your family. Leave time throughout your week for you individually, you and your spouse, and your whole family, where you can do something that's enjoyable. This can be relaxing or fun. For example, reading, hiking or going to the park to have a

spontaneous picnic. Make sure you take time to enjoy your life—you absolutely deserve it!

Our environment is more important than we realize. It determines if we feel happy, organized and successful. It's impossible to feel powerful and successful when you are surrounded by dirty laundry, a stack of dirty dishes in the sink or the smell of a dirty litter box! If you can swing it, I highly recommend hiring a cleaning service to take care of things around the house. I have to admit, when I first contemplated hiring a cleaning service, I felt uneasy. I felt that I wasn't living up to my duties as a wife and mother and that somehow I would be letting my family down. Now I know that that is a load of garbage. We have a maid service that comes every other week and it's awesome! I can now focus on more income-producing activities in the three to four hours it would take me to clean the house each week. In other words, use your time wisely!

Once you focus on structuring your day for success, you will be amazed as to how much time you really have in a day!

Challenge Time!

Challenge #1: What changes can you make to your existing office space to create an environment for success?

Challenge #2: Answer the following questions:

1. Do you have a website that effectively represents you and your unique brand, as well as the transformation you offer?

2. Do you have a hot, compelling offer that your target market will find irresistible?

3. Do you have an opt-in form on your website or an opt-in page?

4. Do you have a list management service to manage your contacts?

5. Do you have a system/service in place to process sales?

Challenge #3: Commit to implementing at least three of my Top 10 Time Management Tips. Then, next week add two to three more. Keep adding them until you are implementing all ten tips!

List the first three here:

_____

_____

_____

Empowering Quote:

"Entrepreneurs have a great ability to create change, be flexible, build companies and cultivate a kind of work environment in which they want to work."

—Tory Burch

Chapter 10

PUTTING YOUR PRIORITIES
AND VALUES FIRST

**Passion Belief Method Step 4,
"Define Your Priorities and Values"**

T ake a moment and think about what's most important
to you in your life. The things that are coming up for
you are your priorities: the people you love the most
in the world and the things you enjoy doing. Finding a balance
between life and work, family and other obligations can be

extremely challenging. With technology so readily available and constant demands from everyone around us, it gets harder and harder to focus on what's truly important. Priorities get clouded as we navigate through our busy days. Deadlines, commitments and to-do lists are never-ending, and before we know it, we are pushing what may be most important to the bottom of our lists.

The first step . . .

Identify Your Priorities

Remember, priorities should be the things in your life you love and enjoy, and also the activities that are going to allow you to reach your goals. For example, the income-producing activities we talked about in the last chapter. The key is to be committed to your priorities no matter what!

Challenge Time!

List five to ten of your top priorities in your life and business.

_____

_____

_____

Defining Your Values in Six Steps

A value is a principle or quality you find intrinsically valuable or desirable. Values are personal; a set of values is so important that a person just doesn't feel right when what he or she is doing is in conflict with one of them. Value conflicts can generate high levels of personal stress. There is no right or wrong set of values, though there are cultural norms embracing certain values as more correct than others.

Your values are the things that you believe to be important in the way you live your life and how you conduct your work. They (should) determine your priorities, and deep down, they're probably the measures you use to tell if your life is turning out the way you intended for it to.

When the things that you do, the choices you make and the way you behave, match your values, life is usually good. But when these areas do not align with your values, things feel "off." This can be a source of unhappiness. This is why making a conscious effort to identify and focus on your values is so important.

When you know and understand your values, you can answer often challenging questions like these:

What career should I pursue?

Should I accept this promotion?

Should I compromise or stay firm with my decision?

It's important to understand that values do not have strict boundaries and they can change throughout your life.

Challenge Time!

Take out a clean sheet of paper and answer the following questions.

Step 1: Think about the times when you were most happy.

- Who were you with?
- What were you doing?

Step 2: Think about the times you were most proud (personal/career).

- Why?
- Were there other people involved? If yes, who?
- Were there other factors involved? If yes, explain.

Step 3: Think of the times you were most fulfilled.

- What need or desire did you fulfill?
- Was it personal or work-related?
- How and why did the experience give your life meaning?
- What other factors contributed?

Step 4: Determine your top values based on those experiences of happiness, pride and fulfillment.

- Why is each experience important and memorable?

Using the list of common personal values (found below), pick ten values that you resonate with and write them down. Some might naturally go together, like happiness and joy.

Accountability	Ambition	Boldness
Accuracy	Assertiveness	Calmness
Achievement	Balance	Carefulness
Adventurousness	Being the best	Challenge
Altruism	Belonging	Cheerfulness

Clear-mindedness

Commitment

Community

Compassion

Competitiveness

Consistency

Contentment

Continuous
   Improvement

Contribution

Control

Cooperation

Correctness

Courtesy

Creativity

Curiosity

Decisiveness

Democratic
   Fairness

Dependability

Determination

Devoutness

Diligence

Discipline

Discretion

Diversity

Dynamism

Economy

Effectiveness

Efficiency

Elegance

Empathy

Enjoyment

Enthusiasm

Equality

Excellence

Excitement

Expertise

Exploration

Expressiveness

Fairness

Faith

Family-orientation

Fidelity

Fitness

Fluency

Focus

Freedom

Fun

Generosity

Goodness

Grace

Growth

Happiness

Hard Work

Health

Helping Society

Holiness

Honesty

Honor

Humility

Independence

Ingenuity

Inner Harmony

Inquisitiveness

Insightfulness

Intelligence

Intellectual Status

Intuition

Joy

Justice

Leadership

Legacy

Love

Loyalty

Making a
   Difference

Mastery

Merit

Obedience

Openness

Order

Originality

Patriotism

Perfection	Self-control	Teamwork
Piety	Selflessness	Temperance
Positivity	Self-reliance	Thankfulness
Practicality	Sensitivity	Thoroughness
Preparedness	Serenity	Thoughtfulness
Professionalism	Service	Timeliness
Prudence	Shrewdness	Tolerance
Quality	Simplicity	Traditionalism
Orientation	Soundness	Trustworthiness
Reliability	Speed	Truth-seeking
Resourcefulness	Spontaneity	Understanding
Restraint	Stability	Uniqueness
Results	Strategic Thinking	Unity
Orientation	Strength	Usefulness
Rigor	Structure	Vision
Security	Success	Vitality
Self-actualization	Support	

Step 5: This step is probably the most difficult, because when you're making a decision, you will have to choose between solutions that may satisfy different values. Therefore, you must know what value is most important to you.

- Refer to your list of your Top 10 values from Step 4.
- Look at the first two and ask yourself: "If I could only choose one of these values, which one would be most important to me?" (Visualize if necessary.)

- Keep working through the list by comparing each value with each other value until your list is in the order of importance.
- You'll have identified your "core values," which will be the first three values on your list.

Step 6: Reaffirm your values.

Check your top values and make sure they fit properly with your life and the vision you have for yourself and your future.

- Are you proud of your top three core values?
- Do these values make you feel good about yourself?
- Would you feel proud to share your top three core values with the people you love and admire most?
- Do these values represent the things that you would support even if the choice would not be popular?

When you consider your values in decision making, you can be sure that you will remain in integrity and be in alignment with what you know is right. You will approach decisions with clarity and confidence, knowing that you're making the best choice for your current situation. Making decisions based on your values is not always easy, but it's always right.

Key Points

Identifying and understanding your values is a challenging yet important exercise. Your values are a central part of who you are and who you want to become. Becoming more aware of these important factors in your life will allow you to use them as a guide to make the best choice in any situation. Some of life's most difficult decisions are really about determining what you value most. When many options seem reasonable, it's helpful and comforting to rely on your values and to use them as a strong guiding force to point you in the right direction.

Values also play a large role in identifying whom you want to work with in your business. I'm sure you can recall a time where you felt uneasy about working with a particular client. Maybe that person was rude or unenthusiastic, but you decided to work with him or her anyway (most likely because you didn't want to pass up the money). That person was not in alignment with your values, so the outcome of the experience ended up being negative.

When you're getting clear on whom you want to work with and how you want to serve them, it is necessary to base this on your priorities and your values, so you can remain in integrity and be fulfilled through your work. Putting your priorities and values first, in everything you do, will allow you to live a life of joy, abundance and peace.

· ·

Empowering Quote:

"Your beliefs become your thoughts, your thoughts become your words, your words become your actions, your actions become your habits, your habits become your values, your values become your destiny."

—Mahatma Gandhi

· ·

Chapter 11

EMPOWER YOUR LIFE BY SETTING
WELL-DEFINED BOUNDARIES

S etting and maintaining clear boundaries is an essential ingredient in any home, career or business. For women, in particular, this can be a difficult practice to uphold. With our caring hearts and desire to please, we are more inclined to stay silent rather than "rock the boat" with a loved one, friend, colleague or client.

Establishing guidelines for how and when you do things in your personal or business life doesn't have to feel like harsh rules and red tape. Boundaries come from having a good sense of our own self-worth. Think of setting boundaries as the way to honor your time, so that you offer the best of you to all of those around you.

First, take some time to set up boundaries. Second, make sure everyone is aware of your boundaries. This way, when issues do arise, it's much easier to take a stand and ask that your boundaries be respected.

Guidelines for setting up boundaries around common issues:

- **Set up your calendar to accommodate your priorities first.** We discussed this in the previous chapter; however, it's so important I want to cover it again here. Creating solid boundaries when it comes to your priorities in life is going to be the key to your happiness. Be sure to first plug into your calendar all of your family obligations and activities, important meetings, trainings and all other things near and dear to your heart. Then, schedule your calendar of events for the times when you will engage in your income producing activities. Next, schedule your marketing and program development time, and finally add content creation time for your newsletter, blogs or social media. This should serve as a guideline for how to prioritize your calendar while honoring your values.

- **Relationships.** Personal boundaries are the limits we set that allow us to protect ourselves in relationships with family and friends. They make it possible for us to separate our own thoughts and feelings from those of others and to take responsibility for what we think, feel and do. These boundaries allow us to rejoice in our own uniqueness. Personal boundaries are flexible—they allow us to get close to others when it is appropriate and to maintain our distance when we might be harmed by getting too close. Good boundaries protect us from abuse and pave the way to achieving true intimacy. They help us take care of ourselves. When it comes to relationships with those who help you with your business, it is up to the coach, consultant or service giver to outline the boundaries as to who's expected to do what and by when moving forward.

- **Work time in your home or office.** Often working in an office with coworkers or working from home can present many challenges in the form of disruptions—staff members interrupting you every five minutes at the office, or your spouse or kids asking what's for dinner. When it's time for you to be focusing on your work, it's up to you to let everyone else around you know not to interrupt you for the period of time that you have blocked out on your schedule.

- **Limit time to spend with a client or customer.** When you are working with clients, it is important to respect your time and theirs. Make sure that you maintain control of the conversation, especially when your client goes off track or babbles on about their story. Also, refrain from the need to overdeliver, with excess content. This is giving your time and gifts away and often overwhelming your client with too much information. Keep it clear and concise, letting clients know up front how much time you have together and what they can expect to be covered during the conversation.

- **Choose to do something only if it allows you to maintain your integrity and upholds your values.** In the previous chapter, you learned how to get clear on your priorities and what your core values are. Make sure that you are deciding to do something only if it is in alignment with your values and is going to take you closer to your goals. It's OK to say no. In fact, in order to live the life you desire, a life on your terms, you must learn how to say no. You don't need to back it up with an explanation, either. If you feel the need to say something besides just "no," you can simply say, "No, thank you, my plate is too full right now to take on additional responsibilities at this time, but thank you, anyway."

- **Payment agreements with a client or loan to a friend or family member.** When setting up payment plans with clients or offering a loan to a friend or family member, make sure that the payment agreement is 100 percent clear. Be sure to outline specific dates when the payments are expected to take place, and for what amount, and the specific method of payment. If there is interest, make sure you let the other person know how much and how that will impact the payment total.

Asking for What You Want

In my coaching practice, I see a lot of damage done because people don't know how to ask for what they want, or don't think it's OK to ask for what they want. Not asking for what you want means you'll eventually resent somebody, and that leads to a lot of strife. Let's talk about how to ask for what you want. To really be successful, you need to understand the difference between asking and demanding, and how to approach different people.

The Importance of Wanting

If you don't know what you want, you'll have trouble getting it and experience a lifelong feeling of disappointment, scarcity and resentment. When you aren't able to express what you want clearly, you'll have a challenge obtaining what you desire. You'll also have difficulty feeling generous about your partner's or others' wants and needs.

In a relationship, asking for what you want in a helpful, nonthreatening way helps both you and your partner understand each other. If you don't know what you want, you won't realize if you achieve it. If you don't know what your partner wants, you can wind up with a false or one-sided solution. This will leave one or both of you feeling unsatisfied, manipulated or overpowered. This often comes down to simple communication.

Being clear about what you want is like putting all the facts on the table, just as you lay all the pieces of a jigsaw puzzle out, so you can see what you're working with and more easily solve your puzzle.

Difference Between Wanting and Demanding

Much of the confusion about expressing wants occurs because there is no distinction made between wanting and demanding. Stating what you want is an effort to communicate clearly, so you and your partner can both be satisfied. Demanding is insisting that your partner give you what you want, without regard for his or her wants and feelings. You can tell the difference because when you are asking, you can handle getting the answer no; when you are demanding, you get upset if what you're asking for is denied. When you ask for what you want, it is a good idea to have a backup plan in case the other person doesn't agree.

The Communication Differences Between Men and Women

Women should know how to ask men for what they want directly, and in a rational, unemotional manner. Men respond much better to "Sweetheart, will you take out the garbage?" than to a whiney "The garbage stinks and is overflowing," or "I have to do everything around here!" The indirect request is a female style of communication that works well with other women, but doesn't work well on men, simply because our thought processes are extremely different.

Men need to learn to listen to women's feelings when they want something. Women do not always respond to a direct request; they do better when feelings are talked about. Saying "I'll do it when the game is over" will be received by a woman as disregarding her feelings. "I'm sorry it's bothering you, honey; I'll take it out as soon as there's a commercial break" will let her know the man cares about her feelings, and she'll be happier and more satisfied with it, even though the result is the same.

The Importance of Knowing What You Want

You may be wondering, why being clear about what you want is so important. Many people have serious trouble knowing what they want, feeling comfortable communicating it, and stating it clearly. They have difficulty creating solutions to their problems, because they do not know what they want, or if they do know, they cannot express it effectively to someone else. We often grow up suppressing our desires, sometimes to the extent of not even being aware of them. Once you become clear on what you want, you must then believe that you can achieve it. That belief is what will fuel your desire to take the necessary action steps toward your goal, resulting in your obtaining what you truly desire.

By setting clear, well-defined boundaries in your life and business, you will be able to increase your focus and productivity. It will also allow you to free up time to enjoy your life and business without sacrificing the things that are most important to you. This is essential to live a fulfilled life and crucial to reaching your business goals.

Challenge Time!

Answer the following questions:

1. In what areas in your life are you not honoring your time, values or priorities? Explain.

2. What new boundaries will you establish in your life and/or business? Explain.

• •

Empowering Quote:

"Daring to set boundaries is about having the courage to love ourselves, even when we risk disappointing others."

—Brené Brown

• •

Chapter 12

A HEALTHY YOU MEANS
A HEALTHY FAMILY
AND BUSINESS

I f we look at the human body as one total unit, instead of separate parts of a unit, we see that all of our organs influence and affect one another. For example, the gall bladder affects the liver, which has an impact on the endrocrine system (hormones, thyroid, adrenals), which affects our energy level and our mood.

You can also incorporate a more complete holistic view of healing, because every part of your life affects and influences every other part of your life. For example, financial worries can promote physical changes in the body that may lead to health issues. And it's clearly true that your health impacts everything in your life. When your body feels strong, it is much easier to focus, and your mood is uplifted and calm rather than stressed or frustrated. You are able to see and receive the abundance of life, and look at the glass as half-full versus half-empty. By the same token, when your body is tired, weak and in pain, it's difficult to see and appreciate life's simple blessings or beauty and the opportunities that may be right in front of you. When you're depressed, anxious, fearful, angry or in pain, it's difficult to get motivated to find or connect with your life's purpose or passion.

In this chapter, you will learn many tools of preventive care and maintenance for your health and vitality so you can have the freedom to choose a full and passionate life. Health is freedom—the freedom to live your life to the fullest, to explore, to move, to laugh and aspire to grow. Owning your value starts with loving yourself, which mean taking great care of yourself.

Healthy Eating

Eating healthy is not about strict diets, rigid nutrition philosophies, staying unrealistically thin or depriving yourself of the foods you love. Instead, it's about feeling great, having more energy, balancing your mood and keeping yourself as healthy as possible—all of which can be accomplished by learning some basic nutrition concepts and using them in a way that works for you.

Nine Healthy Eating Tips to Ensure Your Health Success
Set yourself up for success. In order to have success in creating a healthy diet, taking small, manageable steps, rather than making drastic changes, works best. If you approach the changes gradually and commit to them as you go along, you will have a healthy diet sooner than you might think.

- **Keep it simple.** Instead of being obsessed with counting calories or measuring your portion sizes, think of your diet in terms of freshness, color and variety. This way it becomes easier to make healthy choices. Start by focusing on foods that you love and incorporating some healthy fresh ingredients with them. Your diet will become more healthy, and delicious, in no time.

- **Start slow.** Attempting to change your eating habits overnight is setting yourself up for failure. This sudden drastic change will often lead to cheating or giving up on your new eating plan altogether. Take simple, baby steps, such as adding a small salad with a variety of vegetables to your diet each day or switching from butter to olive oil or coconut oil when cooking. As your small changes become a habit, you can continue adding more and more healthier choices to your diet. Every change matters. The long-term goal is to feel good, have more energy and reduce the risk of cancer and other disease.

Moderation is key. The key for a healthy diet is moderation. You might ask what exactly moderation is and what's considered a moderate amount. That really depends on you, your body type and your overall eating habits. Try thinking of moderation as balance. That typically will mean eating less than you do now. For example, if you eat a burger for lunch, then you can eat a healthy dinner such as salmon and a salad. If you eat one hundred calories of chocolate one afternoon, you can balance it out by deducting one hundred calories from your dinner that evening. You'll want to include a balance of carbohydrates, fat, fiber, protein, vitamins and minerals to ensure that you sustain a healthy body.

Moderation can also mean smaller portions. Serving sizes these days are ridiculously big. When dining out, you can split an entrée with a friend. At home, try using smaller plates. If you're still hungry after a meal, try adding more leafy green veggies or fruit.

How you eat is just as important as what you eat. Here are some suggestions for changing the manner in which you eat:

- Eat with others when possible. This has a number of different benefits, particularly for children—it allows you to model healthy eating habits. Eating in front of your TV or computer can lead to mindless overeating.
- Chew your food slowly. Savor every bite. We often tend to rush through our meals, forgetting to actually taste our food and enjoy it. Chewing slowly will also help

with proper digestion of your food. (I admit that I can improve in this area!)

- Listen to your body. Ask yourself, "Am I feeling hungry or am I really thirsty for water?" During a meal, it's important to stop eating before you feel full. It takes a few minutes for your brain to tell your body that you're full, so that's another good reason to eat slowly.

- Eat breakfast and then eat smaller meals throughout the day. Eating a healthy breakfast can jump-start your metabolism, and eating small, healthy meals throughout the day (rather than the three standard meals a day you're probably accustomed to) will keep your energy up and your metabolism going.

- Avoid eating too late. Attempt to eat dinner earlier and then fast for fourteen to sixteen hours. This will give your digestive system a break. So, in essence, you are only eating when you're most active. This will help to regulate your weight.

Fill up on colorful fruits and vegetables. Fruits and vegetables are the foundation of a healthy diet. They are low in calories and full of wonderful nutrients, such as antioxidants, fiber, vitamins and minerals.

Eat healthy carbohydrates and whole grains. Whole grains, healthy carbs and fiber will provide long-lasting energy. Include a variety of whole grains in your diet. Examples of whole grains you can include are: whole wheat, millet, quinoa, brown rice and barley. Experiment with different grains to find your favorite. Whole grains are rich in phytochemicals and antioxidants, which will help to protect against diabetes, coronary heart disease and certain cancers. Studies have shown that those who eat more whole grains tend to have a healthier heart.

The difference between healthy carbs and unhealthy carbs: Healthy carbs include whole grains, beans, fruits and vegetables. When you eat healthy carbs, you will feel full longer and your blood sugar and insulin levels will remain lower. Unhealthy carbs include refined sugar, white flour, and white rice that have been stripped of all bran, fiber and nutrients. Unhealthy carbs are digested very quickly and cause spikes in blood sugar levels and energy. Include a variety of whole grains in your diet to ensure you're eating your healthy carbs.

Eat healthy fats and avoid unhealthy fats. Certain sources of healthy fat are required to nourish your brain, your cells, your hair, skin and nails. Foods rich in omega-3 fats, called EPA and DHA, are particularly beneficial and can lower cardiovascular disease, help with dementia and improve your mood.

Healthy fats to add:

- **Monosaturated fats** from plant oils like peanut oil, canola oil, olive oil; avocados; nuts (like pecans, almonds and hazelnuts) and seeds (such as sesame and pumpkin).
- **Polysaturated fats** (such as omega-3 and omega-6) and fatty acids (found in fatty fish, such as salmon, herring,

mackerel, anchovies, sardines and some cold water fish oil supplements).

Some other sources of polysaturated fats include corn, soybean, walnuts, flaxseed oils and raw sunflower seeds.

Unhealthy fats: trans fats, found in crackers, vegetable shortenings, some margarines, candies, snack foods, baked goods, fried foods and other processed foods made with partly hydrogenated vegetable oils; saturated fats, found primarily in animals products, such as whole milk dairy products and red meat.

A new perspective on protein. Try incorporating different types of protein into your diet, such as beans, peas, seeds, nuts, tofu and other soy products. This will provide more variety and new options at mealtime. Here are some suggestions:

Beans: navy beans, black beans, garbanzos, lentils
Nuts: walnuts, almonds, pistachios, pecans
Soy products: soy milk, tofu, tempeh, veggie burgers
Avoid refried beans and salted or sugary nuts.

Add calcium for healthy and strong bones. Calcium is not only a key ingredient to having a strong and healthy body, it is also an essential building block for lifelong bone health and many other functions.

Good sources of calcium include:

- **Dairy.** Dairy products are rich in calcium and easily absorbed by the body; these include milk, cheese and yogurt.
- **Vegetables and greens.** Many vegetables are rich sources of calcium, especially leafy greens. Try mustard greens, turnip greens, collard greens, kale, romaine lettuce, celery, broccoli, cabbage, fennel, green beans, squash, Brussels sprouts, crimini mushrooms and asparagus.
- **Beans.** For another rich source of calcium, you can eat pinto beans, black beans, kidney beans, white beans, baked beans or black-eyed peas.

Limit your sugar and salt intake. Sugar causes energy ups and downs and can be responsible for health and weight problems. Unfortunately, you have to do more than reduce the amount of desserts, cakes and candy you eat. Most of the time, you may not even be aware of the amount of sugar you're consuming each day. Large amounts of sugar can be hidden in many of the foods you eat regularly, such as bread, pasta sauce, vegetables, soy sauce, ketchup, frozen dinners and canned soup.

Some helpful tips:

Avoid sugary drinks. One twelve-ounce soda has about ten teaspoons of sugar in it. This by itself is more than the daily recommended limit! Try sparkling water or a small glass of fresh juice instead.

Eat naturally sweet food, such as fruits, peppers or natural peanut butter, to help satisfy your sweets craving.

Watch for hidden sugar on food labels:

- Corn sweetener or corn syrup
- Honey or molasses
- Cane sugar
- Brown rice syrup
- Fruit juice concentrates
- Dextrose, fructose, glucose, maltose or sucrose
- Crystallized evaporated cane juice
- Maltodextrin (or dextrin)

Be conscious of your salt intake. Most people consume too much salt in their diets. Too much salt can lead to high blood pressure and other health issues. Try to limit your salt intake to 1500 to 2300 mg. per day, the equivalent of one teaspoon.

- Opt for fresh (or frozen) vegetables rather than canned vegetables—they're much better for you.
- Choose low salt or sodium free products and cut back on salty snacks.
- Avoid processed or prepackaged food—these products often contain hidden sodium.
- Be careful when eating out—most restaurant food is loaded with sodium.

Drink Plenty of Water

Drinking water is a simple and inexpensive remedy that'll increase your energy, fight fatigue, flush out toxins and assist your body in operating at prime efficiency. The Mayo Clinic recommends that the average adult should consume eight to nine cups of water per day. To avoid dehydration don't wait until you're thirsty before consuming water. Many experts believe that if you hold off drinking water until you're thirsty there's a good chance that you're already dehydrated.

Exercise

Do you want to know what the secret weapon is to boosting your energy and mood and relieving stress? Drum roll please . . .

It's exercise!

Exercise is not just about aerobic capacity or building muscles. It actually has even greater benefits for your energy, mood and even brainpower.

1. **Easing stress and anxiety.** Exercising regularly helps to reduce stress and anxiety. Aerobic exercise releases hormones that relieve stress and promote a sense of well-being.

2. **Boosting energy.** Increasing your heart rate several times a week will give you more get up and go! Start off with a few minutes of exercise each day and then build up to more, increasing your workout program as you get more energy.

3. **Lifting your mood.** Exercise can treat mild to moderate depression as effectively as an antidepressant medication—minus all of those horrid side effects we hear about in TV commercials. Exercise releases endorphins, powerful chemicals in your brain that energize your spirit and make you feel good.

4. **Sharpening your brainpower.** The same endorphins that make you feel better also help you to concentrate and stay focused on the task at hand. Exercise also stimulates the growth of new brain cells and helps prevent age-related decline.

5. **Improving self esteem.** Regular exercise is an investment in your mind, body and soul. When it becomes a habit, you begin to develop a sense of self-worth and empowerment. And, not to mention, you'll feel better about the way you look!

The key is to commit to doing some moderate physical activity every day. As exercising becomes a habit, you can slowly add extra minutes or more challenging workouts. Once you start experiencing the incredible benefits that exercise has to offer, such as your physique improving, more energy and feeling more at peace, that will motivate you each day to continue.

The Incredible Power of Breathing

The way you breathe is the way you live. Full, free breathing is the key to enhancing your emotional, physical and spiritual well-being.

Breathing fully and freely is our birthright. If you watch a baby breathe, you will see an amazing sight. With each inhale, the baby's belly fills up with air like a balloon, the pelvis rocks forward, the legs open. The chest rises and then falls, like a raft on the ocean. This is natural, oceanic "full-body breathing"—the way we were meant to breathe. I learned this type of breathing as a comprehensively trained Pilates instructor,.,and it has been part of my life ever since.

As the breath goes in and out, we feel a connection between the inside and the outside. Through breath, we are connected with all living beings. Breathing is incredibly restorative. It can cleanse us of toxins that build up in our body and the mind. It can help rid us of worries and tensions and bring us back to our true nature and our true place in the timeless universe. Breathing is the most basic and essential of all our activities, and it can also be the most transformative.

How to Take a Proper Deep, Cleansing Breath

Breathe in for the count of five, through your nose, and fill up your lungs from the bottom of your diaphragm. Then breathe out slowly, again through your nose, for the count of five. Do this three to five times to bring your body and mind to a calm peaceful state.

Megan's Super Simple Exercise Tips

Super-Simple Exercise Tip #1:
Make a habit of moving more in your daily life

Even if you are not able to carve out a fifteen- to thirty-minute time slot in your day to run, ride your bike or go to the gym or studio, that doesn't mean you can't add physical activity to your day. If you're not ready to commit to a structured exercise program, think about physical activity as a lifestyle, not as a task.

Think of creative ways to add physical activity to your day.

In and around your home. Clean your house, sweep the sidewalk or porch, garden or mow the lawn with a push mower.

At work and on the go. Look for ways to ride your bike or walk more. You can ride your bike or walk to an appointment or the corner store. Always use the stairs instead of elevators or escalators. Purposefully park at the back of a parking lot so you can get some additional walking in. Walk while you're on break or on your cell phone.

While watching TV. Gently stretch or do some light exercises like sit-ups or pushups or lift weights during commercials. You will be shocked at what you can accomplish! Or try leaving the TV out completely and go for a walk instead.

With friends or family. Walk your dog together as a family, or if you don't have your own dog, offer to walk one of your neighbors' dogs or volunteer at a shelter to walk some of theirs. Jog or walk around the soccer or football field during your child's practice. Go on a weekly bike ride with your family or play a game of tag or kickball with your kids.

Super-Simple Exercise Tip #2: Just get moving!

When most people decide that they should start an exercise program, they go and join a gym, buy costly exercise equipment or plan to work out every day. The problem is, they go to the gym a few times, use the equipment a few times, and soon they lose motivation altogether. Exercise does not have to be all or nothing. Take little steps and set realistic goals. The key is to start taking action, exercising ten minutes a day. Then you can build on that, and your momentum will build up as well. You will soon develop the habit of exercising and start seeing and feeling the benefits, which will lead to progression to the next level.

Take it slow. Start with an activity you are comfortable doing, go at your own pace and be realistic in terms of your expectations.

Go easy on yourself. Are you unhappy with your body? Don't be your own worst critic; try a new way of thinking about your physical self. No matter what age, weight or fitness level you're at, there is always someone who is just like you, who has the same fitness goals as you. Find and surround yourself with similar and like-minded individuals who have your same goals. Take a fitness class with others at the same fitness level as you. Set simple goals that you can accomplish; this will build your confidence up.

Remember that you must love and accept yourself the way you are before you can be successful in making any changes in your life, especially when it comes to your health and losing weight.

Make exercise a priority. One of the best things you can do for your physical and mental health is to make exercise a priority in your life. This will allow you to develop the habit quicker. If you have trouble fitting it into your schedule, make sure you put it on your calendar and/or to-do list. There is no excuse; everyone has at least a few minutes a day to exercise, even if it's just walking around the block.

Expect good days and bad days. Don't get discouraged if you miss a few days; the important thing is to start up again and build your momentum back up.

Super Simple Exercise Tip #3: Make exercise fun
You will be more motivated to exercise if you find activities that you like to do, that are convenient and that you enjoy. Make exercise a social activity. Exercise can be a great time to socialize with friends or meet new people. Working out with other people may be just what you need to stay motivated. If that sounds like you, you can find an accountability buddy!

Think of an activity that you enjoy and combine it with exercise:

- Watch your favorite TV show while on the treadmill.
- Put some of your favorite music on and dance with your kids.

- Take a dance or Pilates class (which is of course one of my favorite workouts).
- Work out with a friend and then afterwards enjoy a movie or a cup of coffee together.
- Enjoy some outdoor activities, like gardening, catch, volleyball or yard work.

Super Simple Exercise Tip# 4: Stay motivated

Making any kind of behavior or lifestyle changes can be difficult. It will take time and effort on your part. And be prepared for setbacks. But soon, as you continue to exercise, you'll start to see the positive changes in your body and an increase in your energy, and your mood will begin to improve. That is what will keep you going. You will develop more strength and more confidence. If you get bored, mix it up a bit or try something new.

Some people hire a professional to assist them with their fitness goals. This can be a great way to have a workout program customized just for you and your body. Your trainer will also be there to push you, motivate you and keep you accountable.

Set goals and rewards for yourself. It is important to set some realistic goals for yourself. When you achieve each goal, it's important to reward yourself. You can treat yourself to a new outfit, a new pair of shoes, a new techy gadget or a night out—whatever fires you up! That is a great way to stay motivated.

Challenge Time!

Now that you learned these Super-Simple Tips, there is nothing stopping you from getting out there and reaching your health and fitness goals.

Think about the changes you would like to see in your health and fitness. Write down your new health and fitness goal for the next six months. Use the SMART formula (on page [52])

_____

_____

_____

_____

Pick one of the nutrition tips and one of the exercise tips in this chapter to implement each day, to start improving your health right away. (You can slowly add more to your daily routine when you're ready to step it up.) Write the first ones down below.

_____

_____

_____

· ·

Empowering Quote:

*"To keep the body in good health is a duty . . .
otherwise we shall not be able to
keep our mind strong and clear."*

—**Buddha**

· ·

Chapter 13

GET OUT THERE, SPEAK YOUR TRUTH AND SPREAD YOUR MESSAGE

Becoming Recognized as a Leading Expert in Your Industry

These days, individuals want to work with someone they not only know, like and trust, but also feel is an expert, someone who can show them how to get from where they are to where they want to be. The big question is: how do you become an expert in your ideal target client's eyes?

Well, there are several ways that you can become such an expert. They all involve setting up a platform from which you can share your expertise in an authentic way, providing value to your target clients in the form of educating or teaching them something that they want to know. These strategies will also help to develop your unique personal brand.

Here are six of my top strategies for becoming recognized as a leading expert in your field:

Speak to Live Audiences

My favorite strategy, and what I believe is the most effective one, is to speak in front of a live audience. This can be at an event, workshop, conference, lunch-and-learn, or even a meet-up group meeting. It can be an event that you personally organize or that someone else organizes and at which you are a featured speaker. Speaking automatically increases your credibility and allows you to become vulnerable, which builds trust with your audience very quickly.

Here are seven tips that will allow you to stand out when you're speaking to a professional audience.

Engage your audience from the start. Listeners want to be actively involved, not bored. Give them a reason to engage. You typically have thirty to ninety seconds to grab their attention. Starting with a joke works for some, but only if they have comedic skills. If this is not a skill that you possess, don't go there! What works for most is to start with a powerful and relevant question. I've seen how this can be extremely effective. It brings your audience into the discussion and helps to set an informal and positive tone. Be sure in the beginning of your presentation to also share a story about yourself that allows you to be vulnerable. This will allow your audience to connect with you on a deeper level. Another technique is to refer to one or two of your audience members by name. (I always make sure I spend some time prior to my presentation getting to know some of the people who are there and whom I might reference later.)

Be animated. The best presentations are given by people who are animated in both body language and vocal delivery. Resist the temptation to hide behind the podium or stand in one place. Here's something to try: next time you speak to an audience of twenty or more, walk among your audience when you speak. Stop and every once in a while put your hand on the shoulder of one of your listeners. (It might help to do this to someone you have met before.) Walking in the audience will not only help you to retain their attention, but also allow for a closer connection, making them feel like you're one of them.

Provide value. Be sure you are addressing a specific problem or challenge that your audience most likely is currently experiencing or has faced before. Then, be sure to offer a solution to that problem or challenge during your presentation. Give them actionable steps that they can implement right away. Also, make sure that you have a clear call to action: what action should they take moving forward if they are ready to take the next step?

Pay attention to your delivery. The delivery of your message is very important. No one wants to listen to a stiff or monotone person. Attempt to have a pleasant vocal quality. There are four main areas to focus on this throughout your presentation: vary the tone of your voice, vary your volume, vary the speed at which you talk and learn to pause when appropriate to create greater impact. Avoid distracting habits. These will often distract the audience from focusing on your message. The best way I have found to identify if you have any distracting habits is to either practice your presentation in front of a friend or family member and have them share any constructive feedback, or videotape yourself and watch the recording. Or you can watch yourself reciting your presentation in a mirror. By catching yourself in a bad habit, or at least becoming more aware of what you're doing, you can learn to break the habit.

Dress the part. Do you look like a leader that others will want to follow? Does your attire make you feel confident about yourself? Be sure to wear clothing that is appropriate to the industry culture you are presenting to, but a little nicer than what your audience is wearing. Avoid distracting patterns.

Keep your content fresh. Avoid sharing the same stories over and over again; mix it up or put a different spin or twist on it. A powerful tool is to weave current events into your presentation when possible; perhaps something that happened that day or week might reinforce the reason for the discussion. Make sure that you modify your presentation to appeal to your specific audience. Another way to keep it fresh is to mention the latest trends in their industry or even in pop culture—this will help to keep your audience captivated.

Practice, practice, practice. Rehearse your presentation! Reviewing your notes will not cut it! In order to be a great speaker, you must know your presentation inside and out, backward and forward. You must know exactly how you will start, what questions you will ask, what stories or case studies you will be sharing, when you will vary your tone and volume, where to look and when, and finally what your call to action is. Rehearsing will help you look and sound more polished and, most importantly, allow you to feel more confident.

These speaking tips will allow you to engage and win over any audience.

Create a Blog, Video Blog or Newsletter

Blogging is a fantastic and easy way to get your content out there and share your expertise with others. The key is to post regularly and be consistent to ensure that you are reaching enough people. Always include a call to action, so your audience has an opportunity to take the next step with you. For example, direct them to your website or a splash page, so they can opt in for your free gift offer. Remember, you always want to be thinking about how you can collect their contact information so you can stay in touch with them.

Another favorite of mine is video. You can create a video blog or a Web TV show where you share tips and strategies around your area of expertise. This is a fun way to connect with your audience. It is often even more effective than the written word, as most people feel that they can connect with you easier and get to know you better if they see you.

If you decide to offer a newsletter, it is best to either have a weekly or biweekly subscription. Again, make sure you're not only providing valuable content, but also making an offer of some sort, even if it's just inviting readers to opt in for your free gift. If you're committing the time to do this each week or every other week, you want to make sure that it is profitable!

Write Articles for News Sites and Professional Publications

Make a concerted effort to write articles pertaining to your area of expertise. Send them in to newspapers and trade journals along with other professional publications and websites.

If you can manage to do this, you will have content to back up your authority in your field. Don't simply write a few articles here and there, but instead commit to regular content creation for a variety of outlets, as it helps build up your unique personal brand faster.

Get Interviewed on Radio Shows and Podcasts

Podcasts are typically a niche-driven industry, making them an ideal way to get your message across to a large number of people.

To get on a radio show or podcast, it's best to contact the host. You can usually find contact information, such as email addresses, on the show's website. Tell the host why you would be a great fit for the show. Don't forget about Twitter, Facebook and other social-media outlets, as you can often contact a radio show host through these means. If those ideas don't work, try contacting past guests who have been on the show to find out how they went about achieving an invite.

Be Active on Social Media

Be sure to create a specific Facebook, LinkedIn and Twitter pages for your business. Commit to posting valuable and educational content daily.

Write a Book Using a Problem-Solution Format

Another strategy for becoming recognized as an expert is to take what have been your most read or best received articles and in a book delve deeper into the subject broached in those pieces.

Keep in mind, the book doesn't have to be long. In fact, with today's readers, shorter is often better. However, the book format does give you the benefit of space to really explore a problem and offer up your solution, which will give you instant authority status.

Be sure to choose the strategies from the list above that resonate with you and that you feel excited about. With consistent application in any or all of these areas; you will begin to widen your influence and gain the trust and respect of your audience.

Being Vulnerable

Another effective way to connect more deeply with your audience and build trust is by being vulnerable.

Vulnerability has never been easy for me. It's no wonder. In order to be vulnerable, you have to be OK with all of you, the good and the not so good. That's the thing about vulnerability that no one likes to talk about. I was always afraid to share my low moments with my audience; for example, the time when I was in an unhealthy personal relationship, when my fiancé at the time was very mentally abusive and I let it affect me so much that I almost lost everything I owned. I felt that if I shared that story, it would mean that I was a failure and it could cause people to judge me. What I have learned over the years, is this: all of the experiences in our lives, good and bad, are just stepping stones allowing us to become who we are meant to be.

I now look at those bad experiences in my life as learning opportunities. Now I am much more equipped to help others who are experiencing or have experienced financial challenges in their lives. In fact, the many adversities that I have personally experienced—such as being a widow at thirty, being a single mom for nine and a half years, having financial successes and failures, dealing with many challenging personal relationships, etc.—really gave me quite an education in life that I can share with others to help them when they are struggling in any of these and similar areas.

Being vulnerable is not just about showing the parts of you that are pretty, cool and fun. It's about revealing what you deny or what you may keep hidden from other people. We all do this to some extent. I bet you've never said to a friend, "I just love that I'm insecure."

But that's the point, isn't it? You've got to love everything if you want to choose to be vulnerable.

Brené Brown once said, "What makes you vulnerable makes you beautiful." Most of us have probably experienced vulnerability by default. We are often either forced into that state through conflict, or we are surprised by it after a time when our circumstances felt more comfortable.

Few of us consciously choose vulnerability. Why? The stakes are way too high. If we reveal our authentic selves, there is the great possibility that we will be misunderstood, judged or, worst of all, rejected. The fear of rejection can be so powerful that some wear it like armor.

Vulnerability is so much easier when you love yourself.

Think about it, when you don't love all of you and you're afraid to show people the less than stellar parts of you, the space between you and vulnerability is like the Grand Canyon. It will take all the courage you can muster up to make the leap across.

But when you truly love all of yourself, you don't worry as much about what other people think. And when you're less afraid of rejection, you step right into that place of openness.

Learning how to become vulnerable doesn't happen overnight; it takes practice. Thank goodness, life will give you plenty of opportunities to consciously choose openness.

There are many benefits to allowing yourself to be vulnerable. When I have chosen to be open, to show my authentic self, my clients have met me there. And when they've met me there and formed that connection, there's nothing we can't accomplish.

With vulnerability, you experience true connection—true love for yourself—and you begin to attract people to you who are inspired by your openness.

While it's not easy to be vulnerable, you'd be surprised how loving all of you and then sharing it with another can help you to connect with anyone. In my own life, I'm continuing to open up to my clients and others. It is something that I will continue to work on. I strongly encourage you to do the same.

Challenge Time!

Pick two of the strategies covered in this chapter that you will use to start becoming a leading expert in your field.

_____

_____

_____

What can you do that will allow you to be more vulnerable?

_____

_____

_____

Empowering Quote:

"Leadership is based on a Spiritual quality; the power to inspire, the power to inspire others to follow."

—Vince Lombardi

Chapter 14

KEEP TAKING INSPIRED, CONSISTENT ACTION

Getting out there and spreading your message, "speaking your truth" like we discussed in the previous chapter, can sometimes feel a bit scary. In fact, it often brings up many debilitating emotions within us.

It saddens me to see business owners unable to grow their businesses because they are paralyzed by fear. The truth is, there is no way to eliminate fear in your life—it will always exist.

Eleanor Roosevelt is one of my most favorite leaders from history. She became a leading woman politician of her day.

In 1921, her husband, Franklin, was struck with polio. With that in mind, Eleanor organized Democratic women to help Franklin be elected governor of New York in 1928 and then president four years later. Eleanor was incredibly influential in shaping the Universal Declaration of Human Rights when President Truman later appointed her as delegate to the United Nations. She said, "You gain strength, courage and confidence by every experience in which you really look fear in the face. You are able to say to yourself, I lived through this horror; I can take the next thing that comes along. You must do the thing you think you cannot do." She also learned that "No one can make you feel inferior without your consent."

The only way to grow as a person, a business professional and a leader is to step outside your comfort zone and face your fears, doubts and the limiting beliefs you have about yourself. The key is to have your *why* be bigger than the fear. What is your why? Ask yourself *why* you want to be successful. Your purpose is your why. If you're thinking, "I want to be successful so I can make a lot of money and pay off all my bills or be rich"—it's got to be more than just about the money. Think of what the money would represent, the lifestyle it would allow you to have. When your why is bigger than your fear, you will do the thing that scares you most anyway. And each time you do it, I promise you it will get easier and easier. Also, when your why is big enough you'll figure out *how* to achieve your goals.

I personally have learned to get comfortable "being uncomfortable." For example, I do things that scare me and empower me, such as skydiving, trapeze flying, race car driving, zip lining, speaking in front of large groups, shooting videos, investing a lot of money in myself and my business and, my latest, starring in my own Web TV show. I do these things because over the years, I have learned this is the best way for me to keep up-leveling my life and my business.

I have created a formula for you that will help you move past your fears.

The Five Steps to Conquering Your Fear

1. First, acknowledge your fear and make the decision to face it.
2. Trust that you will get through your fear and become stronger and more confident because of it.
3. Take action. Do the thing that you are fearful of.
4. Assess your feelings. How do you feel?
5. Celebrate your accomplishment!

Fear truly is an illusion we create in our minds. I once heard it referred to as, False Evidence Appearing Real, which makes a ton of sense!

The Power of Taking Action

We've all have heard about the law of attraction. Think about what you want and visualize it, and then you can achieve it or attract it into your life. But many people sit around visualizing their goals and the dreams of what they want to achieve and wonder why they aren't getting any results.

What is missing is the key ingredient, which is action! In order to be successful, you must take action, and not just any action, but inspired action, action that is inspired by your why. And then, take that action consistently. That's how you get results.

The only difference between those who drive toward their goals and get what they want in life and those who can't is confidence. Once you truly realize just how capable, talented and amazing you are, that belief, along with a calm, faith-based sense of certainty, is the key ingredient in truly realizing your value and having others realize it, too.

I would like to share my secret formula for success with you.

Megan's Success Formula

When you have a strong belief in yourself, your why, and your products or services, then you will start taking action steps toward your goal. By taking action, you will begin to get results. The results may seem small at first, and that's OK. You may even have some so-called "failures." That's OK, too; think of them as learning opportunities. After getting results or learning from your mistakes, you will gain more confidence. With your newfound confidence, you will have a stronger belief, and with that stronger belief you will take bigger action, and with that bigger action you will get bigger results. With your bigger results your confidence will soar! And the cycle continues.

In Chapter 1 of this book, I shared a pivotal time in my life that demonstrates a great example of how powerful your belief, or your why, can be. Following the loss of my first husband, I had struggled with the fact that my job required me to be on the road quite a bit. I felt extremely guilty being away from my son, who was only two and a half years old at the time. I made the conscious decision to quit my job and start a business from home, where I could set my own hours and be there for my son and not have to miss out on any part of his life. It was incredibly scary to quit my job, and give up my health insurance, but my why—why I wanted to be successful (to create a lifestyle that put my son first)—was so much bigger than the fear, I did it anyway. I experienced much success and even tripled my income that first year in business. It's amazing what we can accomplish, if we focus on our why.

Because of my dedication and commitment to taking daily, consistent action toward my goals, I've been able to achieve many successes in my life and in business. I now encourage you to let your why drive you to keep taking inspired, consistent action toward your goals. There's no limit to what you can achieve!

Challenge Time!

Think of one thing in your business that you would like to do, to get out there in a bigger way, but for some reason fear is holding you back. Write it down.

_____

_____

_____

Then, follow the five steps above to defeat and conquer your fear once and for all!

Capture your experience below:

_____

_____

_____

· ·

Empowering Quote:

"Don't desire anything you don't expect. Expect it. Know it is happening from your deepest core."

—**Ray Holliwell**

· ·

Chapter 15

BECOME ALIGNED TO YOUR PURPOSE AND ADOPT YOUR NEW PASSION BELIEFS

I n this chapter, I am going to bring everything together for you. **The Passion Belief Method** is my five-step method to your empowered self. This method encompasses everything that is required to become aligned to your purpose and live a passionate, fulfilled and abundant life as an empowered and confident leader. It's how to become the best version of yourself.

Near the beginning of this book, in Chapter 3, you learned **Passion Belief Method Step 1, "Recognize Any Self-Sabotaging Beliefs."** These are the beliefs that are holding you back from reaching your true potential and are ultimately sabotaging your success. Then, you discovered how to let go of the beliefs that are no longer serving you, **Passion Belief Method Step 2, "Let Go."**

In Chapter 7, you learned how to **"Clarify Your Passion/ Your Gift,"** which is **Passion Belief Method Step 3.**

In Chapter 10, you experienced **Passion Belief Method Step 4,** process to **"Define Your Priorities and Values."**

And finally, we have **Passion Belief Method Step 5, "Adopt Your New Passion Beliefs."**

I have created eight passion beliefs that will become your new healthy and empowered belief system, a belief system that will allow you to become the best version of yourself.

Below are my **Eight Empowering Passion Beliefs** for you to adopt to create and develop the "new empowered you."

Your New Passion Beliefs

1. **I offer tremendous value.** I know what I offer has great value and makes a difference in the lives of others, and I deserve to get paid what I'm worth!

2. **I have an empowered relationship with money.** I have a healthy relationship with money. Money is a reward for my services. I know that money makes me more of who I am. I am confident when it comes to

making and managing money. I can do great things with my money.

3. **I am worthy of love and acceptance.** Everyone, including me, deserves to be loved and accepted no matter what; after all, we are all God's creations.

4. **I am a gifted and talented individual.** God has blessed me with amazing gifts, talents and skills that I can use to make a difference in the lives of others.

5. **I am a confident decision maker.** I make decisions with ease and confidence now that I can base them on satisfying my values and moving me closer to my goals.

6. **I deserve to live a prosperous and abundant life.** I will follow my passion and serve others, and in return I will be rewarded greatly with many blessings in my life, for which I will be extremely grateful.

7. **I am a leader that others will follow.** I can confidently and effectively guide others successfully on their path to success by utilizing my skills and talents.

8. **I have a strong desire to follow my dreams.** My passion fuels my drive and desire to take consistent action in moving toward my goals.

Review Time

The Passion Belief Method—Five Steps to Your Empowered Self

Step 1: Recognize Any Self-Sabotaging Beliefs. These are negative beliefs that you have or have had about yourself that will sabotage your success.

Step 2: Let Go. Experience an exercise that will allow you to let go of the "disempowering old you" to make room for the "empowered new you." Follow the three-step letting go process.

Step 3: Clarify Your Passion/Gift. Get clear on what exactly your passion or your gift is.

Step 4: Define Your Priorities and Values. Identify the core values and priorities in your life.

Step 5: Adopt Your New Passion Beliefs. Discover the eight passion beliefs that you can adopt to create and develop your new empowered self.

Four Keys to Living Your Purpose

Once you align with:

1. Your true self
2. Your passion/gift
3. Your priorities
4. Your values

then, and only then, can you begin to live your purpose. When you are living your purpose is when you will feel the most fulfilled. That is when your life will become effortless and things will begin to flow with ease and grace.

I have experienced much struggle in my life. These were times when my life was out of alignment. For example, when I was at an all-time low—when I had lost almost everything I owned in a very unhealthy relationship—everything seemed to be going wrong and I was completely miserable. I made a conscious decision that I didn't want to be unhappy anymore. I didn't want to struggle financially anymore; I didn't want to be in a loveless and abusive relationship anymore. I got really clear on what I didn't want, and then it was time to get clear on what I did want. At that time, I did a lot of soul searching. I got connected with my true self and started to focus on what made me happy, what I was passionate about. I identified my priorities (the things that were most important to me) and the values that I wanted to uphold in my life.

I realized that my true passion was to work with entrepreneurs and to assist them in creating a profitable business around their passion and to serve others with their gifts. I knew that I wanted to keep a flexible work schedule, so that I could be there for my son Cameron, and create a lifestyle where I could live joyfully and abundantly, all while serving others with my gifts. I wanted a life filled with love.

This vision of my new life and business was crystal clear in my mind. I was so excited about my new path. I began mapping out a plan for my vision and started to take the necessary action steps toward my goals. I began listening to my intuition and used it as a guide to help me discern what next steps to take. I was called to attend a retreat at my church, which ended up being an amazing cleansing experience for me, giving me the opportunity to address some deeply rooted emotions, from the painful loss of my first husband, that I had subconsciously tucked away. The experience was incredibly liberating. Of course, I still struggle from time to time with the loss of my husband, as I miss him very much, but now I know how to deal with the emotions that I'm feeling, instead of burying them away.

Six months later, I attracted my wonderful, loving second husband, Andrew, along with his two awesome daughters, Lauren and Ashley. We got married two years later. What a blessing it has been. I never knew I would become a mother of *three* amazing children. I am now living a life that many only dream of. All because I took the necessary steps in getting into alignment with my purpose.

I often work with clients who are feeling guilty for following their passion and their purpose. For most of their lives they have chosen to ignore their passion, the fire burning inside them, because they felt that if they followed it they would be neglecting their family and not properly fulfilling their role as a spouse and mother.

If you have that burning desire to be or do something more, then you must honor it. If you don't, you will be left feeling empty and unfulfilled, living a life of regret and possibly resentment.

There is no better gift you can give your children than to be a positive role model, to be a living example of what is possible. Show them firsthand that you can accomplish anything that you set your mind to and that you can be successful by following your passion and doing what you love.

When you are happy and fulfilled, it reflects in your mood and attitude, and your family will get to experience your joy. You will be able to share quality moments together with your family, where you can support one another in a positive way, with each of your individual goals and with your collective goals as a family.

Creating Your Legacy

You can choose to follow your dreams and be an inspiration to others. This is the legacy you can leave others when you leave this earth.

Legacy is more than something that is left behind after a person has passed. Legacy is about sharing what you've learned and not just what you've earned, and bequeathing values over valuables, as material wealth is only a small fraction of your legacy. I feel the true meaning of legacy is when you are genuinely grounded in offering yourself and making a meaningful, powerful and lasting contribution to humanity by serving a cause greater than your own, serving others by sharing your gifts with them, ensuring that you embrace your uniqueness and passionately immerse your whole self into life, so that your gifts will be for all. You will take responsibility to ensure that your gifts will have a life beyond yours, their creator, outlasting your time on earth. How will you live out the fullest expression of yourself?

When you own your value and earn your worth, you will have the ability to give back in an enormous way. Here are a few examples: You will give back through the valuable service that you are providing by sharing your gifts. And as your business grows, you will require more support, which means hiring team members to assist you in your mission. In this case, you are able to provide jobs for others, so they can provide for themselves and their families. The more people you serve, the more money you will make. You can then share that money with people in need. You can contribute to causes that are near and dear to your heart. I support a nonprofit organization that I love, called Spirit Reins. Spirit Reins is a ranch that assists children that have experienced trauma, abuse or neglect in their lives. The ranch offers unique trauma-informed therapy services involving horses, to provide these children with hope and an opportunity to rebuild self-esteem, self-confidence, self-control and trust. They offer a second chance for these families. I am honored to be part of such an amazing organization (www.spiritreins.org). You can even create a foundation of your own that supports a cause that you believe in.

You see, when you are living your passion and your purpose, you can ultimately make a significant impact in the world, one person at a time.

I want to share a story about my son, Cameron, whom I'm incredibly proud of. Cameron is one of the most unselfish people I know. I would love to take credit for this, but he was like this since the day he was born. Many of us like to refer to him as an "old soul." Cameron, now seventeen years old, has made decisions in his life based on putting others first. He is an extremely positive person and always wants to help others. He became an Eagle Scout at age fifteen, completing all of his required Boy Scout levels in three short years. He decided to dedicate his Eagle Project to a place called Florence's Comfort House in East Austin. This is a safe place, where underprivileged children can go to get love, food, shelter, and guidance with their homework. Cameron's project was very extensive and consisted of gutting and rebuilding a food pantry, building a cat shelter and landscaping and building a tepee for the children to play in. In order to raise funds for the project, he organized a run in our neighborhood, called Flo's Fun Run. In addition to the funds raised from the run, he also found other donors and local business sponsors to help fund the project. Once the funds were raised, he gathered a group of Scouts and friends to assist in the project, which he managed. The final outcome of the project was amazing. Flo's Comfort House was transformed into an even better place for these children to feel safe and get cared for.

For his incredible leadership over the last several years Cameron has been recognized with countless awards and accolades. After attending college and getting his degree, he plans on serving his country and being commissioned as an officer in the Air Force. His goal is to lead a Pararescue Team. (Which scares his mama to death!) He has felt a calling to serve his country in this manner since the age of ten. (Who am I to stand in his way?) He has been preparing for this role over the last seven years. He is currently Junior Class President, Second in Command, of the JROTC Program, a Student Council member, a National Honor Society member, on the Student Advisory Board as the Community Service Committee chair, on the Principal's Advisory Board and a mentor in the PALS (Partners in Learning Success) Mentorship Program. As you can imagine, I'm very proud of him. I know he will continue on this path and accomplish great things in his lifetime, making this world a better place.

The reason that I am sharing this with you is that I learn every day from my son; he teaches me how to be a better person and reminds me to put others first. I am blessed.

It also reminds me to continue on this journey that I am on, to believe in myself and keep taking inspired action, sharing my gifts with the world.

· ·

"Be courageous, take inspired action and share your gifts with the world."

—Megan Tull

· ·

· ·

Empowering Quote:

"If you know when you have enough, you are wealthy, if you carry your intentions to completion, you are resolute, if you live a long and creative life, you will leave an eternal legacy."

—Lao-tzu

· ·

My Free Gift to You

. . . .

Discover what your **Passion Belief Factor** is…
Take my **Passion Belief Method Assessment** Today

Discover where you stand when it comes to:

- Your self-worth
- Your value
- Your relationship with money
- And the level of passion in your life and business

This assessment is designed to guide you in understanding yourself better, so you can begin to craft the life of your dreams. To claim this exciting gift, simply go to our website at

pbmassessment.com

Follow these easy steps:

Enter your name and email address. Next, enter this **Special Access Code: PBMROCKS** Finally, answer the simple question provided and then click submit. You will instantly be directed to the assessment. Once your answers are submitted you will immediately receive your Passion Belief Factor score including detailed analysis!

SPECIAL OFFER #1
PASSION BELIEF METHOD
EMPOWERMENT CARDS

. . . .

Get your very own set of empowerment cards featuring
the eight Passion Beliefs from the Passion Belief Method™
Go to: **megantull.com/success-tools**

My Gift to You: Save 20% by using Coupon Code:
PBMSAVE

SPECIAL OFFER #2
YOUR CHANCE TO DIVE DEEPER

. . . .

Passion Belief Method Coaching Program

Are you tired of struggling and not getting the results in your life and business that you know you are destined to achieve? Are you ready to put an end to the self-sabotaging behavior that's preventing success in your life? If so, it's time dive deeper and take the next step. You can finally become in alignment with your passion, values and true-self. With "*The Passion Belief Method*™" Coaching Program you'll gain the confidence necessary to catapult you forward as your "new empowered self" and finally be able to reach your true potential in your life and/or business.

For more information on this program:

Go to: **pbmcoachingprogram.com**

Use Coupon Code: PBMSAVE

and receive 20% off the program tuition!

ABOUT THE AUTHOR

Megan is an Entrepreneur Success Strategist; an in-demand Certified Business and Life Coach, International Speaker and Transformational Leader; and the CEO and Founder of Silverlining Concepts, LLC, a business coaching and consulting firm that offers innovative and transformational programs and workshops for small to mid-size companies. Megan offers a life-changing message showing her clients how to create the income they desire while living an authentic, joyful life based on balance and self-care.

A lifelong student of personal and business development, Megan brings to her work a powerful entrepreneurial background, one that exemplifies perseverance, talent, ingenuity and an "outside the box" thinking mantra. Recognized as one of the top trainers in the United States for the highly competitive health and skin care industry, she was brought in to transform and revitalize the sales teams of three of the top spas in the country, and in the process increased their yearly sales quotas by an average of over 30 percent! After tragically losing her husband and the father of her only son at the age of thirty, she was determined not to be a victim. She made a promise to herself to make the most of her life and her entrepreneurial passion and set out to achieve personal and financial goals and objectives most would have found daunting. However, by increasing her focus on financial freedom and success, Megan tripled her income in twelve months with her first home business. She has started up and run seven successful businesses and has been an entrepreneur for over twenty-five years.

Megan now lives in Austin, Texas, is married to the man of her dreams and has an incredible blended family that includes three amazing children. She loves nature and enjoys running each morning with her husband and her dog, Flopsy. She also adores horses and loves to go horseback riding as often as possible. She is passionate about giving back and is involved in many non-profit organizations. Megan is also a comprehensively trained and certified Pilates Instructor and enjoys practicing and teaching Pilates. She is a thrill seeker and loves to participate in any activity that gives her an adrenaline rush such as, race car driving, sky diving, zip-lining, trapeze flying, public speaking and participating in anything scary or haunted!

She is living the life she teaches others how to create for themselves, a life of faith, love, joy, health, abundance and prosperity. She's living proof that with a lot of faith and persistence, and getting clear on your purpose, dreams really can come true.

Megan's clients and audiences walk away with valuable information, strategies and tools that they can utilize immediately to improve their business and personal relationships and business and leadership skills, taking themselves and their business to the next level.

Megan has helped shape and change the lives of thousands of individuals, and business professionals as a Life and Business Success Coach, Fitness/Pilates Expert and renowned speaker. For more information go to www.megantull.com or email support@megantull.com.

Acknowledgements

I have been blessed with amazing love and support throughout my personal and professional journey.

I would like to share my heart-felt appreciation to...

I would like to first and foremost thank God. Thank you for giving me the peace in being certain of my path. And for my strong desire that burns inside me every day that allows me to stay committed to my path.

My wonderful husband and partner in life, Andrew, thank you for your unconditional love and always supporting me in my dreams. For your patience and understanding during the long hours I spent working on this book. I love you with all of my heart. Thank you for the memories...the best is yet to come.

To my incredible children, Cameron, Lauren and Ashley, you are my greatest joy. Thank you for your understanding during the last year and a half as I created this book.

Cameron, you are my light, thank you for teaching me how to be a better person.

Lauren, I'm so proud of the young woman you are becoming.

Ashley, thank you for your caring and loving messages you send me each day. Keep sharing your beautiful gift of singing with all of those around you.

Thanks to my twin sister and best friend, Monica. You are always there alongside me encouraging me and supporting me in everything that I do. Thank you for being my soundboard anytime I want to run ideas by you. You've been such a blessing, I'm so grateful to have you in my life.

Thank you Mom and Dad. Mom, thank you for your love and belief in me. Dad, thank you for being an amazing example of human kindness; your caring and generous spirit touches everyone you encounter. Your unfaltering positive attitude inspires me each day. I know the distance between us is great but both of you are always in my heart.

A special thanks to Mom and Dad Tull. I'm forever grateful for welcoming me and Cameron with loving open arms and for all of the times that you have helped out with the kids. And thank you for providing your amazing editing skills and valuable input during my writing process.

Along my path to success I have worked with some amazing coaches and mentors that by sharing their wisdom and expertise I've been able to grow exponentially both personally and professionally.

My deepest gratitude to Ruth Klein, without you I'm certain that I would not have gotten this far. You helped me realize my dream of writing this book and your guidance during the creation of my book proposal was spot on. Thank you for believing in me and all of your positive energy and words of encouragement. You are an inspiration to me and so many others.

I'm so blessed to have so many incredible friends that have been there for me through thick and thin. I appreciate you all cheering me on as I took on my goal of writing this book. Your friendship is a treasure that I will always cherish.

To my photographer and friend Amy Weisson, thank you for your masterful photography skills. The pictures that you took were awesome. Thank you for making me look so good!

To my editor Richard, thank you for your brilliant editing skills and catching all the imperfections!

Thank you to my new family at Morgan James, I'm honored to have the privilege of partnering with you on this journey. Terry Whalin, it was because of you that I was certain that Morgan James was the best fit for me. You all have been so incredible to work with your professionalism and commitment to my book has been unwavering.

Last but not least, to my amazing clients, thank you for allowing me to be your partner in success and live my passion through assisting you. I'm so proud of the level of commitment and dedication you bring every day, as you take action toward your goals. I'm honored to be there to experience your incredible transformations in becoming the best versions of yourselves and realizing your true potential in your life and business.

CPSIA information can be obtained at www.ICGtesting.com
Printed in the USA
BVOW11s0046141115

426801BV00002B/1/P